LYING FULLY CLOTHED

Exposing The Naked Truth About Men

DEAR ROB

authorHOUSE®

AuthorHouse™
1663 Liberty Drive
Bloomington, IN 47403
www.authorhouse.com
Phone: 1-800-839-8640

Published by AuthorHouse   04/10/2012

ISBN: 978-1-4678-9059-5 (sc)
ISBN: 978-1-4678-9060-1 (e)

LYING FULLY CLOTHED

Contents

Introduction

Firstly, I am no saint and do not profess to be one. I am not Mr Holy . . . G-d knows me. Whatever you do in the dark will always come out in the light—call it the Vybz Kartel effect.

I can admit that I have been 'that arsehole' who a lot of women wished they had never met. I'm not, in any way, shape or form, proud of the many hearts I have disabled and shattered along the way—but, as they say, for every broken heart there is a guy with a glue gun.

It was my insecurity that led me to behave in such a manner; I wanted to flatter my own ego, not considering the repercussions this could have had on others.

I would promise things that I knew I could not do; which would go to prove the theory that all men are dogs. Needless to say, not all men are dogs and neither do all men cheat (I just thought I'd clear that up). In trying to impress my friends and be the top *strike-her* in my team, I ended up messing around so many girls.

I would sleep with women I could tell were broken, because I knew they would view me as a tower of refuge—and with my myopic vision I couldn't *see how* I was making it worse for them.

The key to any lasting relationship is to under-promise and over-deliver. There is no point you promising her the world but buying her an atlas.

I have near enough done and seen it all when it comes to girls. I've slept with friends of friends, slept with three girls in one night—*on* the night—and

I've even had threesomes. They say good things come in threes, but I regularly use a condom—call it a hat trick. It's funny how men are labelled players whereas women are labelled hos. However, I guess we do live in a world where double standards reside.

While on my mission to inflate my ego I 'farked up' with the best woman that ever waltzed into my life. If you ever have a queen in your hand, don't shuffle; you might end up with a joker. It was the realisation of this that allowed me to rethink my ways. In my exuberance to chase the cat, I got my own stuck up a tree. I was in a relationship with a woman who was giving her all but I wasn't giving anything. At times, as humans, we take things for granted. One must appreciate what is in front of you before it turns its back on you. I would commit to things that I knew were impossible to achieve—telling half-truths amongst half-truths. I over-promised and under-delivered. She received an atlas. They say you don't know what you've got till it's gone—and *boy* . . . she left and now I know the saying's right.

Anyway, enough of the sob story.

I decided to write '*Lying Fully Clothed: Exposing the Naked Truth About Men*' to help shed some light on the psyche of the male species. I have come across many women (no pun intended) and it became apparent that a lot of them like reading horoscopes but have problems seeing the signs. I guess some women have never had that 'hero-type' older brother or father figure in their lives to explain what the majority of men are like.

The most peculiar thing is that I never actually intended to write a book. The title of being an author was not something I wished to add to my CV. The genesis of this book came about through conversations I had with women who would ask me for my opinion regarding men. They were aware of my background; they knew I'd been the guy they would have wanted to run a mile from. The global village also played a large part in my decision—from the many Tweets, to the countless Facebook status updates, an influx of messages would arrive from women asking for my advice on their partners.

My advice usually worked in their favour, which most were a tad shocked to discover. Because so many women were partial to my views on relationships, they requested I start blogging, which I did. It was the success of my blogs that has, in effect, led you to reading this book.

I was usually brutally honest with my views and experiences, sharing information on how some men think about situations. I am not one to give a woman a sugar coat when it's cold; I'd rather the cold breeze freezes her nipples and shocks her back into reality. I am not one to tell a fairy tale. I am not one to stroke a woman's ego. I say it exactly how it is. The fact that I have dealt with so many women and spent a lot of time with the boys, I can therefore give first-hand accounts based on the thoughts and actions of the men I have spent time with. A lot of men who talk on differences between men and women have never been that guy; never been the asshole that you wish you never exchanged bodily fluids with. Well, fortunately for you, I have. This book will give you a primary account on how to avoid swine, and most of the subjects addressed will be straight from the horse's mouth.

I was raised by my **mother** (I've put her in bold letters because I want her to stand out. My **mother** is the closest thing I have to G-d), the giver of life. My father 'legged it' so quickly I thought Usain Bolt may have been my dad. Damn! He left with speed.

The only thing my dad taught me was how to survive, and that is because he was not there. When it comes to single parent household dynamics, I have been there; when it comes to witnessing male-to-female domestic violence and the effects it has on the woman and the child, I have been there. I have the scars on my legs from the beats I received from my mum, which stemmed from her frustration with being stuck in an unhappy DV relationship with my dad.

Relationships are as difficult as the people involved make it, and it seems that a lot of women simply don't understand the X chromosome. From conversations I have had with many guys, it is evident that we are not actually complex mammals. We are not.

This book will be a medium to help uncover and undress any fallacies or preconceptions that you may have about men.

In writing '*Lying Fully Clothed: Exposing the Naked Truth About Men*', I decided to study Anthropology in order to gain an insight into the human body and its workings. I wanted to find out what triggers us, as humans, to behave the way we do. This, coupled with my own knowledge and personal experiences with women, and also the vast amount of people I interviewed, helped in putting this book together.

So if you are a woman who has had sleepless nights trying to figure men out, this book is for you. If you are a woman who would like to give your daughter unadulterated advice about men—this book is for you, too.

The Dirty Games Men Play

"Men play the game; women know the score."
                                        —*Roger Woddis*

Why Do Some Men Like To Play Games?

Well, I guess it's a case of 'mind over matter'. We men have behaved in such a way that it has caused many a woman to have their backs up against the wall. Our behaviour as men, which stems from the primitive times, has inadvertently forced women to build a barrier so that no man can hop over to try and pinch a petal off her flower. Misogynistic men, over time, ostracised women so much that the moment they got what is deemed as equal rights, they threw their aprons on the floor and said, "Fark you, scramble your own eggs and make your own sandwiches."

Women's status has forever been a social quagmire; she has always been a foxy manager of men; she has always capitalised on a man's stronger sexual urge, for her own interests and to her own advancement. By trading subtly upon her sex charms, she has often been able to exercise authoritative power over man, even when she was held by him in forlorn slavery.

Both sexes have had great difficulty in comprehending each other. Men find it hard to understand women regarding their strange mixture of ignorant mistrust and fearful fascination coupled with suspicion and contempt.

1

The stories of Eve, Delilah and Pharaoh's wife (who tried to tempt Joseph) has not helped in trying to enable men to trust women. These narratives were always distorted to make it appear that women brought evil upon man. All of this encourages the universal distrust of women.

Stories such as Eve and Delilah have not painted women in a good light. Christians tend to blame the fall of man on Eve. But, if anything, we have to ask why Adam was so docile that he could not think for himself. Truth be told, I do not believe there was a "fall of Man"—but we shall not digress.

Men have forced women to act the way they do, which has in turn caused men to exercise their game playing. The tricks and manipulations are in response to how women originally acted to the way the men treated them in the first place. Confused a little? Remember, energy is never lost; it is merely transferred.

Okay, Dear Rob, Enough Of The Ramble Already. What Are These Games?

Don't, for one second, think that a man waiting one month to have sex with you means he is a gentleman; get that thought out of your head this very instance. Most men before meeting you (not all) were probably stroking someone's cat. When he left your house, he most likely went to Sandra's afterwards; the reason he didn't move to you when he came around was because he just *buss* juice minutes before getting to yours. Under no circumstance should you equate a man not wanting to sleep with you as him being a gentleman. You making him wait doesn't mean *ish* if he is getting *punash* elsewhere.

A lot of men have already learned the best way to get the cat is to not chase it, because chasing may just get it stuck up a tree. I come to you in the name of Zangeif, don't judge a man's character on him not wanting to sleep with you. Yes, some men may want to genuinely wait, but they are an anomaly.

Game #1: Bareback Riders

A lot of men 'Bareback Ride' because they have problems getting it up—their instrument likes to play Floppy Joe; that split second from going to get the condom and putting it on, can result in their man dying. So what do some do? They play the sex roulette of life and put their coin into your slot machine. But, hey, it seems like some of y'all don't mind.

Oh, and be very careful in doggy style position; many a man has taken condoms off when turning you around. Yes, you're right, that wasn't all your cum—and yes, you're right again, that's how you got pregnant.

Game #2: I Need To Keep on Top But I'm Looking For A Base

Ladies, if you have your own place and he doesn't, be very cautious. Some men target women with their own place so they can use it as their base; their place to do all the dodgy dealings they do. Don't be that girl that allows a man to hold things in your house; don't be that naïve broad. Some men are looking for women with their own place so they can try and wiggle their way in. First it's the toothbrush, then you start seeing letters in his name and I'm not talking about the ones on the fridge. A drowning man will clutch onto anything to save himself. A man, who is on his face, needs you.

Game #3: I'm Trying To Make A Change. Can I Bank On You To Take Note?

Under no circumstance, I don't care how good his hood is, should you ever lend a *link* money. What for? Why can't he go to his boys? Has he burnt his bridges with his family, so he's looking to cross one with you? I come to you in the name of Prophetess Beyoncé, don't do it! The way you will fight tooth and nail to get your money back will be a *mudting*. Yes, there are some men who may give it back but with the stories I have heard, they are in the minority.

Why, in the name of fruitcakes, would you take a car out on finance for a guy you are linking? Explain yourself. Come on, ladies, this love thing seems to confuse you a little too much. Many a man have done this to women and ducked, no daffy.

Game #4: Yeah, Babe, I'm Going Out Of Town For Business

That's nice; in fact, that's great. A man who works out of town has always got an excuse not to be at home. Men who are self-employed cannot be traced time wise because at any given moment he may be on business. Is he too fucking busy or is he too busy fucking?

Game #5: Is He Into Me Or Not?

If you have to question this, then he's either not interested in you or he's playing games. If the answer is the latter—it's *long*. If a man is playing so many games that he's left your heart in no man's land, is he really the guy you want around you? The problem is that many women in their head, from the get-go, think: *he has to be my man!* and they overlook all of the things he does because they just want it to work. If his feelings for you are on JSA, there is no point. All of this '*How do I know a man is into me?*' is not necessary. If a man is into you, he is into you. Men are not indecisive by nature. The moment you have given him the cat (and he is enjoying it) you should give him no more than three months, max, to make his mind up. Was he indecisive when he was putting his male member inside you? You ladies shouldn't be too full on; I know some of you like to be when applying make-up but this isn't the canvass for that.

If a man takes your number and it takes him a week to call you, I'm sorry but he is *not* that into you! Unless a great travesty has occurred in his life. (Or, possibly, he's playing games . . .)

If you call a man in the day and he calls you back the following day, unless he has a really plausible excuse, like he was wanking—he is *not* that into you. (Again, he could be playing games . . .)

You're in the same rave as him, and he knows you're there, and he is entertaining other girls—he is *not* that into you.

Some men will flirt with your friends as an attempt to get you jealous; it's the reverse psychology we play, and most of the time it works.

Game #6: How The Fark Did He Know I Have A Tattoo?

Well, well, well, if you know what is good for you do not send pictures of yourself to a link with your face in it. If you do, just know it's likely the whole team will be ogling over your pictures for free. And believe me-you some of these pictures have been sent to men in jail for them to, ermmm, yeah—let's just say the baby oil isn't only to moisturise kneecaps.

Sex tapes are great but as a woman you need to ensure that *you* have hold of it; just know, if, and when, it goes sour it will be sweet for his team to view. I have seen many pictures and videos of women, yes I have.

That's why his friend was so on you; he knows you have a good head on your shoulders and knows you know how to *suc*-ceed.

Game #7: Hey, Babe, Why You Clapping?

Those headaches weren't headaches; let's just say the other chick's head was banging, no migraine, and he accidentally slipped his medicine inside. Dude got given the clap, so therefore he couldn't sleep with you until his dose had run its course. What man doesn't want to have sex? Let's be real, come on now.

Watch out for him trying to use the kids as an excuse. He might go and pinch little Dante in his sleep, bring him into the bed just so you don't have to 'get it on', Marvin Gaye style.

Game #8: Errrmmmm, Babe, Your Mum's Butters

Watch out for those 'Jedi Tactics'. Your man might just come home one day and cause an argument. Yup, some men do this, especially on the weekend when they want to go out. Yup, randomly he might just attack something you've been doing for *time* simply so he can go out with the lads, or, even worse, with his *Sweetcorn* (side chick).

Oh, and might I add when a man is constantly picking holes at you, whining and moaning, more time he is feeling guilty because he is 'cheating'. Watch out and pay attention. It is a defence mechanism that some men use.

Okay, Dear Rob, I'm Depressed Now

Men and women are regarded as two distinct varieties of the same species, living in intimately close proximity. Their viewpoints and life reactions are essentially different. I believe they are wholly incapable of full and real comprehension of each other. Complete understanding between the sexes is not achievable.

Men will tend to play games as will women. The Battle of the Sexes is one thing that has been here from the beginning of time. Women seem to have more intuition than men, but they also appear to be, errmmmmm, somewhat less logical. Women, however, have always been the moral-standard bearer and the spiritual leader of mankind. The hand that rocks the cradle still amalgamates with destiny. The key is to use your brain and not your heart when dealing with men. The best thing you can do is be yourself—and before settling down with any guy, introduce him to the men in your life that you trust. Let them scrutinize him; it's important. I can smell a rat from a mile away.

If you're looking for a man to complete you,
you've missed the whole point.

Ten School Girl Errors And Common Misconceptions Women Make In Regards To Men

"Here's all you have to know about men and women: women are crazy, men are stupid. And the main reason women are crazy is that men are stupid."

—*George Carlin*

Error #1:

Stop making excuses for a guy's shortcomings; you trying extra hard is not going to make up for what he is lacking. YOU'RE JUST GOING TO BURN OUT. Putting icing on shit will not make it a cake.

Error #2:

Men are different from women. You need to accept this fact and deal with it. If not, there is always *JLS*. You can't judge men by women's standards

Error #3:

Stop pretending; be who you are. Let us see the real you. Most men are not pleased by the fake; stop trying to please—it will not make us anymore attracted to you. Most men are not attracted to women who kiss up to them. If you have to suck up to him (no fellatio) you're probably barking up the wrong tree. Keep barking up the wrong tree and the birds will soon shit on your head.

Error #4:

Don't share your feelings too early. Good-looking men are very well versed; we have experience, we know what to expect. One thing that sends us running is a girl who, after a couple dates, says "I really like you. I can see a future with you." It indicates you're the clingy type, or one who jumps into relationships quickly. Don't do it; lean back and relax. Acting too eager will show that you are desperate.

Error #5:

Stop relying on your natural instinct to figure us out. You bra-wearers communicate differently, like flirting, showing silly signs, playing with your hair (body language). Us men tend to use sarcasm, our wittiness, even cockiness. Very rarely will men be able to communicate how they feel; hence you have to learn how to read body language. And pay attention to our behaviour.

Error #6:

Do not expect a relationship to make you happy; if you are naturally a depressed, sad, sorry individual then '4 gerrit', you are slightly delusional. Nothing will make us run more than realising a woman wants us to take care of her. If you are not bringing anything to the table you will not eat. As much as we want to make you smile, we're not looking for a liability.

Error #7:

Why oh why? Do not try and persuade a man to like or love you. What the hell for? You will never be able to persuade a man on how he thinks about attraction; we have different tastes. If a man isn't feeling you, how do you expect him to do so with reasoning? Like: "Umm, excuse me, err, I'm a really lovely girl, really pretty," so therefore he should take that on board? Hell to the mf no, you're out of luck. The computer says no, no, no and no again. (However, men are the worst at this: showering women with compliments even when trying to get their number; or is it their BB pin or fuck book? We still do it as men, even though we know it won't make most of you like us.)

Error #8:

Don't think because you are aesthetically attractive that every guy you meet will want to settle down with you. GALACTIC FAIL. From the get-go a man will know what he wants from you, and I don't just mean putting his coin in your princess purse. If you jump in expecting this dude to want to settle with you, you will be pleasantly embarrassed. Men are not indecisive by nature. Think back to when you were younger and you asked your dad something—when it was a "maybe", "don't know" or "not sure", did it ever materialise? Think back with your ex—when you asked him something and it was a "maybe", "don't know" or "not sure", did it ever materialise? An indecisive answer, in most cases, means NO. Ask him if he wants fellatio and watch how clumsy he gets; watch him drop his briefs.

Error #9:

Don't be scared to ask for help; there is nothing more annoying than a proud woman. We do not like it; it lets us know you're a woman who is pompous and will not back down from an argument. Yes, we have eyes and can see you have a space saver wheel on your car, but can you open that mouth of yours—that you're ever so used to running—and ask for help? Many thanks, amen, cheers.

Might I add, there's a difference between asking for help for something you want and something you *need*. We're happy to help with the latter; for the former, we may not be so forthcoming. Keep that in mind.

Error #10:

Making a man wait months on end will not necessarily make him take you serious; that is a myth from the deep jungle of Zamunda. It is a lie; we are more interested in your character. You telling us "Oh, I want to wait until next time" does not impress us; it doesn't. Your character is important; so important. You sleeping with us in the first week does *not* constitute you being a slag, it does not.

It's important that you grasp this: even if you make a man wait a month, it doesn't prove anything, because eight out of ten times the dude was sleeping with someone else before he met you. So before he came to yours he most probably went to Sheila's, stroked her cat and then came to yours. Most men are like snipers; they can sit in the cut and be patient. If he is getting sex elsewhere, he can wait until you're ready. If you think fasting your cat will make a man take you serious, good luck.

The most important thing is that you've had "that chat"—I will elaborate on this further on in the book.

If you're looking for a man to complete you,
you've missed the whole point.

Where Have All The Good Men Gone And Where Do I Find One?

"Women cannot complain about men anymore until they start getting better taste in them."

—*Bill Maher*

What Happened To All The Good Guys?

What happened to all the Dillons (good guys)? *You* did—yes YOU, YOU that's reading. You ignored Dillon; you used him for emotional intimacy without reciprocating, in kind, with physical intimacy. You laughed at his consideration and resented his devotion. You valued the aloof sex God man than the attentive 'just-a-' friend.

Dillon would follow you here and there; he would be the shoulder to lean on. Your friends would tease you about him and say how he fancied you and you'd just shrug it off. He'd be the guy who would take you shopping, the guy you called before beefcake would come round and sex you up. You took and rinsed Dillon emotionally—yes, rinsed him. You told him about the other guy; he'd sit there and listen. He would lend an ear to hear.

Given Dillon's behaviour was a bit wet, you passionately denied any romantic feelings for him. You completely denied any feelings for him because he was a bit short, too dark, not the right size, blah, blah, blah. Eventually this platonic prick *'got the got'* in his canoe and got the drift.

12

Then your boyfriend cheats on you or the relationship becomes stale because Dillon's extra support and care on the side is gone, so emotionally you're empty. You realise that the things that attracted you to that beefcake weren't exactly the things that sustain a relationship.

So you're SINGLE again, waltzing through bars, and then ask that famous question: "What happened to all the good guys (Dillons)?"

YOU BLODDYCLART DID.

You mocked his consideration, his thoughtfulness, you laughed at the fact he was saft like squidgy breast, you mocked him behind his back, you resented his devotion. Dillon now realises that women must not be attracted to guys who hold open doors; guys who do all that I have listed above. A guy who cooks for the sake of it, a guy who is attentive, a guy who you can share your inner most feelings with.

He came to the realisation that for him to get a woman he'd have to act like your beefcake man you always complained about. So he turns into him and starts getting punani, treating women the same way you described beefcake to him.

I'm sure we've all watched the program 'Take me out'—whenever a guy came on who was an accountant, lawyer etc., the girls would turn their lights off. *'A wadi back foot to bumba'*. What the fark? Why the hell are they turning their lights off? They would also turn their lights off if he had a close relationship with his mum. Watching that programme gave me a clear indication that a lot of women actually like to cry. Yes, some of you must have shares in Kleenex because it doesn't make any udder tucking sense.

You're Looking For A Nice Guy?

HERE'S WHAT YOU DO:

1) Manufacture a time machine.
2) Go back a few years and stop being a wedgie and pull your head out your ass.
3) Take a look at what is in front of you and grab it.

I guess the other possibility is that you actually don't want that nice guy, but you still feel the social pressure to at least pretend you have matured past your infantile taste in men. In which case, you might be in luck, because Dillon has shed his nice guy Mantle and is out there looking to unleash his pessimism onto someone like you—if you were five years younger.

A woman will most likely only come across a handful of 'nice' guys in her life.

SO, EITHER STOP MISREPRESENTING WHAT YOU WANT, OR OWN UP TO THE FACT YOU FARKED YOURSELF OVER—AND, NO, MY CAPS LOCK BUTTON ISN'T STUCK, I AM SHOUTING.

You aren't getting older, after all; excise the bullshit and get to reality. Stella does not always get her groove back

Okay, Fark You, Dear Rob, I Admit I Farked Up A little . . . How Do I Redeem Myself?

I will start by saying this: the same approach will always bring the same results. You can't plant banana and expect to get mango—nope, sorry, it isn't happening. Only an insane person would think that attacking a challenge in the same way will bring different results.

Switch up your game, stop going for the same guys. It is apparent that it is these same guys who keep breaking your heart, so why in the name of Kunle and George do you keep going back—are you Oliver Twist? Do you just *like* to cry? Why do you keep falling for the same type? Break the mould.

Look at your get up. The way you dress will more time determine the sort of men that will speak to you. You are the marketing force that drives your campaign.

It's high time some of you women start introducing your potentials to your real male friends so they can scrutinise them properly. Stop using your intuition alone; it is clear it hasn't got you that far.

If you've gone for the same kind of guy once, twice, and it didn't work, why are you going back to the same prototype? Seriously, I actually question the thought process of some women. I know it sounds harsh but some of the guys you women go for are ridiculous.

Enough Of The Ear Bashing. Where, If Anywhere, Do We Look?

A rave is the last place you want to be looking. Up until this day, I have still never heard a man say "Let's go raving, I feel like dancing. I really feel like shaking a leg." Yeah, your third leg. I'm sorry, in the urban raving scene, I am confident enough to throw a blanket over this statement and say: "Men do not go raving to solely dance." No, we do not. We go to draw numbers—no Picasso.

I've seen Christian girls break out in the spirit when bashment comes on; every scripture they have ever read became redundant. Soon as bashment comes on, the inner whore in many a woman comes out and all thoughts of wifey flies straight out the window.

Look at the dynamics of a club: lights are low, alcohol flowing; most women dress like prostitutes, men acting like pimp-daddies, seductive music playing in the background, women gyrating. Add all these elements together and you've got sexual innuendos violently flying about.

The first thing most men are thinking when they see you is: sex sex sex and more sex. He more than likely just wants to bang. I have never made a girl I met in a rave my Missus, and I know many a man who haven't. When most men go raving, they are looking for Ms Right now, not Ms Right. Of course, there are exceptions. Some people have met their loved one in a rave, but those are anomalies.

How long have you been raving for and what joys has it brought you apart from bags under your eyes and a *brukk* pocket?

But Where, Dear Rob, Where Do I Search? I Like Skinning Out To Dumpa Truck

Start going to seminars, conferences, debates, property auctions—as stupid as this may sound, this is where you are more likely to find affluent men. If you are of a certain calibre, this is where you need to be heading. Go to shows that they hold at London Excel; places where you are dressed appropriately and sex is not on the agenda. When a man sees you in a professional environment, he may think sex but he may also think *Wifey*.

Don't get me wrong, good men *do* go raving, but the vast majority will not wife a girl they meet in a club. The agenda, more time, is sex and it will be very hard to convert him. No man likes a woman who consistently raves. If he does, lift up his skirt and check what he's got down there. That whole slutty dressing that the club dictates does not help in any way shape or form. Men are visual creatures; that alone should tell you how one should dress.

Do not think for one second that going to church will change anything... As much as it is a church. A sinner is a sinner—yes, there shouldn't be any sexual innuendos floating about but it's imperative to use precaution. Some men go to church to devour Christian sisters; I know this first hand.

It seems to have been deemed a faux pas for guys to *chat* you up on the road when you are on your way to work. This is one of the best times to give your number out, as this man is seeing you in your formal wear. There is nothing sexier than a woman who knows how to make money; as long as you aren't Oprah, **balling,** but then again some men like to see women **cry.** The same way women like men in uniform; we like to see women in uniform, too. Let's get out of this 'low donkey' syndrome: if a man is coming correct, give him the time of day.

Supermarkets are a great place to meet people, they sure are. Have a wander down the ready meal isle; you're bound to find a man down there. But just make sure you haven't got any ready meals in your trolley, as that might work against you; no man wants a woman who can't cook.

Weddings, christenings and even funerals—yes, I said funerals. These functions are places you women need to be taking advantage of. Family functions and gatherings where men can be verified and checked over. A lot of you women tangle with men and haven't even run any checks on them. There are men you fark and there are men you keep. It's for this reason why I admire Jada Pinkett. For those who don't know, she used to do a thing with Tupac back in the day. But did she have any kids for him . . .? No. Did she settle down with him . . .? No. Who did she settle down with . . .? Yep, Mr Big Willy Smith.

Learn from this, ladies; please learn.

Jada Pinkett took the dick for what it was and left it there. A lot of these men are only good for farking and that's where it should stay. They say "you can't turn a ho into a housewife", so why would you try and turn a scrub into a husband? She knew what she wanted from a man and she got it.

Lauren London on the other hand . . . Oh my heart bleeds for her. Why did she go there with Lil Wayne? Like, seriously. I am flummoxed. A man with multiple baby mamas, countless felonies, and a history of womanising—what is the bloodyclart meaning? And then she will say "all men are dogs". There are men you fark and there are men you make sure you never get pregnant for. *Darnit*, I used to love this girl . . .

In closing

There are good men out there, but sadly they get passed over because they don't look hip or fly. Where has hip and fly got you up to now? It's okay, I can wait.

You can't attack problems the same way and expect to get different results. It isn't going to happen. It is asinine to assume it would. Start frequenting places where men with clout go; go to places where sexual innuendos aren't on the agenda. Less raving is a must. I am yet to know of a man who has said: "Let's go dancing tonight."

Be honest with yourselves. Why do you dress the way you do? What are you trying to incite in a man's head? Let's be honest for once and excise the **Britney S**pears.

There is nothing wrong in meeting people off social networking sites. There isn't. It isn't hard to build up a rapport with somebody and it isn't hard to check mutual friends. Are you saying that meeting someone in a rave is any better than on the internet? Really? If you aren't too sure about meeting him alone, invite him to a bar or a show where your friends will be. People use social networking sites a lot but if you have pictures of yourself in a provocative manner—once again, all he is likely to be thinking is sex. Certain women need to stop presenting themselves as a **tool** for sex; or all he'll want to do is **screw drive-her.**

Oh, and shout out to all the Facebook models who have to pay photographers for shoots. If you were a real model, you wouldn't be paying for shoots. Just admit you like to pose semi-naked.

Yeah, this chapter has been a bit harsh, but sugar-coating, at times, covers up the real message.

If you're looking for a man to complete you,
you've missed the whole point.

From The Number To The First Date

"A gentleman is simply a patient wolf."

—*Unknown*

Somehow this jackal has persuaded you to give you his number, and he wants to **meet** you even though he's **vegetarian**, so now you're just sitting there, hoping he doesn't make a **meal** of things.

Now, before you even anticipate meeting up with said dude it is imperative that you get to know a few things about him; what I like to call "the fundamentals". It is essential that the two of you have *that* conversation; you know, the one that opens the both of you up and allows you to explore each other's personalities. First dates can be daunting, especially when you haven't got peace of mind. It is very important to settle yourself, so that when you do eventually meet up with him you are comfortable to a degree. I chortle to myself when I hear some women say they would never go to a man's house on a first date as they don't deem it safe. But it's funny how the majority of these same girls will expect him to pick them up from their house and drop them home. So this same guy knows where you live and, also, who's to say he couldn't drive you to a hilltop to a nice bit of scenery and attack/rape you there if he wished? If you aren't sure about said dude, should you really be meeting up with him in the first place? Ponder on that for a hot minute.

As stated, one must settle their mind first before meeting up with him; at least settle *yourself* so that you can feel free and relaxed on the first encounter. There are some things you will need to find out about him to make sure that you aren't wasting your time.

Something which I call C.O.C.K: Culture, Occupation, Credentials and Kids.

Culture

Now, if the dude is from **Poland**—and, as much as we all like a good **polish** from time to time, if you don't want to date someone from that country, is there any point with the two of you meeting up? Most men are not in the game of throwing away **watches**, so don't waste our **time** or yours. We can pretend and try and be PC but culture plays a big part when it comes to dating.

Some are very lax when it comes to this, but their parents may not be. So before even venturing out on a date, one should at least get to know his ethnic background.

Also, along with culture comes religion. We have many different faiths because of culture. If you look at world religions you will notice that most regions have their own religion. If you are Christian and he is a Muslim—you're going to meet a **hurdle** that even **Colin Jackson** may have problems leaping over. It's a shame that the Abrahamic religions claim exclusivity and their route being the only way to paradise. If you are a member of any of the three Abrahamic religions (Judaism, Christianity and Islam) you shouldn't really want to date somebody out of your religion, as when it comes to judgement day, if you *do* make it to paradise, they won't be there with you. That's if you believe in the concept of hell, which you should if you are a true believer of either one of these faiths. In addition, if the two of you were to get serious you may find that your views may clash when it comes to the raising of your child. Furthermore, would your parents approve of you getting married in a Church if you're a Muslim? Hmmm, food for thought.

The funniest thing is that if you put a Jew, a Christian and a Muslim in the same room, all three would swear that their religion is the one; well, you all can't be right, two of you have to be wrong.

If you're opposed to getting with a guy from a particular culture—or a man who is religious or not religious, as you may be an atheist or agnostic—it's good to get these things out of the way to avoid awkward moments, like when your weave's itching but you can't pat it because he's sitting in front of you.

Occupation

Yes, we can sit here and pretend like a man's occupation doesn't matter, but for most of you ladies it *does*. It's good to know what the dude you're intending to meet up with works as for a living. If you're opposed to dating someone who moves food (sells drugs) like a Tesco lorry driver, it's good to try and get these things out of the way. I can imagine some of you saying: "Do you think a guy is really going to say he sells drugs or does fraud?" You'd be surprised; some will. If a man earns money illegally, it is likely he will say he is a businessman or make up some story as to how he earns it. He will be very vague, may even say something along the lines of "Just know I make money."

He may be a male stripper for all you know; if that be so and you are opposed to that occupation, there's no point in the two of you meeting up.

If you are earning, let's say 50k, and he is earning, let's say 20k, you may find that the difference in salary may cause a huge problem, as the places you frequent and can afford may be different to the places he can, so it may be a good idea to gauge what kind of man you're dealing with. Suggesting going to Claridges might give him a mild case of angina.

Credentials

Find out his qualifications; find out what achievements he has accomplished. Find out whether the two of you are on the same wavelength mentally. Does he live at home with his parents? If so, what are the reasons behind this? Does he drive? If not, why? Yes, we can sit here and pretend like some of these things don't matter, but it *does* to a number of you. Save yourself the aggro of going on a date and wasting his time by finding these things out. There was one girl who met a guy on holiday; he was in his thirties. They started dating when they got back to London—only for her to discover he shares a bunk bed with his thirty-five year old brother. Yes, I said bunk bed, and the killer is that he dumped her because he felt that she was putting too much pressure on him to change it. Can you imagine? The said dude allegedly wanted to stroke the cat while the older brother was on the top bunk. Now, not saying that where a man is in life should amount to the be all and end all of your decision in meeting up with a guy, but it would be naive to suggest that we as humans don't have some sort of a tick list; if things like, a man not having a **driving license,** puts you off, then **d**on't **v**enture **l**ying **a**bout the matter. Should you really waste your time meeting up with him? But in saying that, should that really stop you—are you that shallow?

In this new age/culture that we live in, where we see many people getting harassed on that programme called 'Boarder Force', it is in your best interests to also find out what this dude's status is. Now, I am not saying that you should ask this prior to meeting up with him, but if he somehow slips it in his sentence that he is on a work visa or something; on the lines of he-has-no-permanent-residency-in-the-UK—that should get your alarm bells ringing. Dude might want to use you to get his papers, and I am not talking about A4. Yes, there are people out there who will get with a woman/man just to get their stay and bounce like Spalding. I wouldn't advise any woman to get with a man who has no stay unless he's looking to give you some surety upfront. Some of these people get paid sums of money, like 8K, to do an arranged marriage. Don't let a man get a free ride off you.

Kids

Yes, kids, those lovely cherubs that bring joy into our lives. If he has **three BMs** and none of them are **German vehicles**, this might be a turn off. It's better to find this out before clipping in your weave, attaching your eyelashes and putting on your spanks. If you are opposed to dating men with kids, there is no point wasting his time or money. One thing that I have found, though, is that a lot of guys lie about having kids. Yes, some men deny their kids in search for the cat. So, once again, even if he tells you *I have none* it is imperative to still do your own research; believe-you-me many a man will **stand up** and **lie** on a **mattress** at the same time about not having kids or about the amount of kids they have.

Also, a man who doesn't check for his kids is not someone you should be considering as a potential partner. Yes, he may have what he deems a legitimate excuse, but as far as I am concerned there is no reason as to why a man should not check for his kids, none. Irrespective of what may go on with him and the mother of the child that should not affect the relationship with him and his offspring.

If you're looking for a man to complete you,
you've missed the whole point.

He's Not A Drug Dealer
But He Ticks A Lot Of Boxes

"There are two perfectly good men:
one dead and the other unborn."

—Chinese Proverb

Let's assume that you've had that conversation with him and he's ticked all the boxes you require to be ticked. What next? Time to get your glad rags on and meet up with him.

Now there seems to be set of women who are opposed to going to a man's house on the first date. Some seem to think that we men will deem you easy. *Easy*? For coming to my house? Why would I think you were easy? Does you coming to my house mean we are having sex? Does it give me automatic access to Sheba? If you don't want to go to a man's house because kitty hasn't been fed in a while, and you don't want to get tempted, then by all means stay clear away until you feel ready and comfortable to do the do. If you claim that you are hungry and I say that I am cooking and you say that you don't want to come to mine because you don't deem it safe, I will retort with: *should you even be meeting up with me in the first place if you don't feel safe*? As stated earlier, if your reason for not wanting to come to my house is because you don't want to be in an intimate setting with me, then cool, say so, but don't reply with: *it's not safe*. It's more than likely a man will be picking you up from your house, so are you saying it's safer for him to know where you live? Think about it logically. It's not by force that you must go to a man's house on the first date; it is not, do what you're comfortable with, but if he does invite you around, the excuse of safety or not feeling comfortable may put him off, especially if you said you were hungry and he replied by saying he was, or is, cooking.

Now, before meeting this guy, let someone know where you are going and who with. Now that we have social networks it's not hard to put a name to a face. I implore you, whether it is a friend, family, or the dog Benjy, let someone know who you are going to see; just in case he is a weirdo, like those people who still support Arsenal. I feel sorry for the kids who they force to wear their Jersey; it borders on child abuse. So yes, the address of where you're going should be given to someone for the *just in cases*. And also, it would be good to even let the chap know that someone is aware that you are in his company by merely having a conversation with someone briefly while you are with him.

You've Gone To His House

Let's assume you've gone to his house for the first date; it would be a thoughtful gesture, if he is cooking, to bring a drink along or some sort of dessert—but in saying that, the way certain men enjoy drinking from the furry cup *you* may actually *be* dessert. But yeah, bring something along; it will put you in a good light. Now, if you've had that conversation with him, you should feel a bit at ease as you now know his C.O.C.K. By this point, you should feel like you know him a bit; the fundamentals. Bear in mind that you will never ever get to fully know someone, as time is not stagnant and people do change. But at least you've got to know a few things about him. Assuming he has cooked for you, you could return the gesture by offering to wash up. Asking to help shows signs of thoughtfulness; once again it will put you in a good light. If your intention is to make this dude your man, seeing as it is the first date, I would advise you to not let the cat out of the bag—with some men this may not favour you. However, be advised, if he has already done his HPI check on you and it comes back bad, you can make him wait two months and in most cases it won't make a difference. But as a general rule of thumb, I would say avoid sleeping with a guy on the first date. Even if it means going to his when the decorators are in town—yes, I know some of you girls do this on purpose. Don't try it with me; I'll tell you to show me the string or I might start feeling around your ass to see if I can feel the pad—I kid, I kid. But yeah, avoid sleeping with a guy on the first date; it's a no-no. What may be running through most guys minds is how many *other* men you've slept with on the first date. Anything after the first date is a free for all; do as you wish. If we have done our check on you and it's come back clear, it should be all systems go.

You've Decided To Go Out

As I've stated, if your real concern is that you didn't want to go to his house because of your safety then you shouldn't want him to pick you up from your place—and you really shouldn't want to enter his car. Surely you wouldn't want him knowing where you live, and you wouldn't want to enter the big bad wolf's car now, would you? If that be the case, and you're not sure about said dude, then make your way to the designated location and feel free to make your way back.

Now, in deciding where to go, don't opt for the cinema or theatre on your first date. How do the two of you intend on striking up a conversation in the cinema/theatre? Unless you plan to go for drinks after, it makes no sense. So you go cinema, it finishes, and you go home—you might as well have not met up as you haven't actually tried to build up a rapport. Even if he suggests going to the cinema, explain to him why you'd prefer going somewhere else in a subtle way. But not like a mum; don't be condescending.

Some men are beta males—they are not very good at making plans and aren't very proactive (Dillons). If that be the case opt to go out to a bar or some sort of relaxed setting where both of you can feel comfortable. I would suggest avoiding going to dinner as this can often be a bit pretentious—and from talking to many females about this issue, some of you find it a bit daunting. And talking with food in your mouth isn't too sexy either. I once took a girl to a restaurant in Westow hill called Joanna's. The waitress poured a small amount of wine in her glass so she could taste it to see if she liked it; the girl was looking at the waitress like she was crazy, wondering why she'd only poured a li'l amount in her glass. I chuckled inside so much I think my cheeks below my spine released gas slightly. The funniest thing is that the girl was acting all prim and proper. She was all using the teaspoon to eat her dessert—it was ridiculous. So yes, try and avoid restaurants as much as possible. Attend a nice, cool, calm setting where the two of you can simply gauge each other out. It could be a trip to a museum; it could be anywhere. Remember, YOU are the date; it's your company that is most important. The place you go is simply the location. YOU are the date.

Now let's get this clear and out there like big tits in a small bra: it is not written anywhere in stone that a man must pick you up from your house and drop you home; it is not, so feel free to eradicate that myth out of your cranium. A man does not have to make four trips. Is his first name Benson? As in pick you up from yours, take you to the location, drop you home and then drop himself home. And to be fair, if the date has gone bad, it is better you get your own method of transport so you don't have to depend on him dropping you home. As much as it may be deemed chivalrous for a man, he is not **Donald Trump**; he doesn't have **to pay** on the first date. Yes, it may be nice but it is not set anywhere in stone that he must. I have heard many times that it's the person who invites the other party out that pays. Well, in the majority of cases, during the early stages, it is the man who does this most of the time—so are we saying that the man must pay all the time? Are you an escort? Is that your reason for not attempting to pay for at least one of the dates? These sorts of things will leave you in a bad light with most men.

Just in case the date goes wrong, it is important you bring your purse with you (your vex money) or you may find yourself in the back, washing dishes, and we wouldn't want you to chip your *purty* nails. Also, if the date goes wrong and you're not fond of his company you don't have to endure going through the whole date, you can simply jump in a cab—that's if you haven't driven—and make your merry way home.

Now, if your date is not a pertinaciously odoriferous individual and you feel like giving him a kiss—why not? Do it. That's if you want to. Don't be pressured or persuaded in doing so. However, if you are in his house, he may see it as you teasing him, so I would advise you to keep your lips to yourself. If you are out and you're going home, yeah, why not pucker up those bad boys? Put some lip gloss on them and give him a nice wet one. But keep it short and sweet; short enough for him to want some more. It's always good to end the first date on a buzz.

If Prince Charming has decided to drop you home; if he is thoughtful, he will wait for you to actually go inside your house. Unless you live in Peckham or Brixton, then the main road will suffice. You can make your way from there. I jest, I jest.

It is common courtesy to check if he has got back in safely if he dropped you home; unless his name is Addison. Just a simple text to say, "I really enjoyed tonight, hope you got back okay". Something as simple as that could make a whole heap of a difference. If you've both gone your separate ways from the location of your date, a thoughtful man will text/call to see if you've got back home safe. If not, he might have gone to his other link's house to stroke her cat. Yes, don't for one second think that this doesn't happen; it does, my **dear**, ask **Bambi**. (Or, another possibility, is that he's playing games.)

If you're going to make a man pay on all the dates, the least you can do when he comes to yours is cook him a meal. Jheeeze.

If you're looking for a man to complete you,
you've missed the whole point.

PRIDE

The Biggest Cockblock Known To Man?

"We allow our ignorance to prevail upon us and make us think we can survive alone, alone in patches, alone in groups, alone in races, even alone in genders."

—*Maya Angelou*

Well, well—that dreaded word: *pride*. That thing that can make you think that the light at the end of the tunnel was a train, when in reality it was a man wearing a helmet with a light on it coming to help.

What Is Pride?

According to the Oxford Dictionary, pride is "the quality of having an excessively high opinion of oneself or one's importance".

Of all the hazards which plague man's transient nature and imperil his spiritual integrity, pride is the greatest. Courage is heroic, but egotism is vainglorious and suicidal. Reasonable self-confidence is not to be condemned. Man's aptitude to transcend himself is the one thing which separates him from the animal kingdom.

Pride can be fallacious, bewildering, and sin-breeding whether found in a person, a group, a race, or a nation. It's true when they say: "Pride goes before a fall."

One of my favourite quotes from *The Art Of War* is "Pretend inferiority and encourage his arrogance". Chomp on that for a second.

Now, one could say "What is wrong with having a high opinion of yourself and of one's importance?" The problem arises when you think you are better than others, so then you harbour contempt for those around you.

One thing I always say is: "If it's perfect you're looking for, take a look in the mirror and tell me if you see it. If you do, practice **safe sex** and **do one.**" Nobody who walks the earth's surface is perfect. We are all trying to perfect our imperfections.

You are your greatest invisible foe, which can be manifested in four different ways: Anger, Pride, Deceit and Greed. Man's greatest victory is the conquest of himself.

You Know It's A Wrap
When She Goes Out And Buys A Cat

I come to you in the mighty name of Ashwarf of the seven seas and treacherous clouds, don't let your pride leave you on the shelf. This pride some of you women have is almost depressing. How can you ask of a man to do more for you, than you can do for yourself? Are you taking the Michael Stevenson? You want a man with a Beemer, Benz or Bentley, when this time all your money can reach is a Skoda, Daewoo or a Uno. Let's be real, this is why some men call women *gold diggaz.* You are a *gold digga* if you are looking for a man to do things for you that you can't even do for yourself. If you, as a woman, can, then all you're doing is trying to find someone on your wavelength which is fine. This pride is a real real *real* cock blocker. Cut your cloth according to your size.

Many times I have been out and I have seen girls with their face push up, like to say they've been baptised in lime juice. Why are you mean-mugging? What is the meaning?

Do you lovely ladies know how much courage it takes to actually come and lie to you? I mean speak to you? (Honest typo.) I really wish the tables could turn so you *wombman's* could see what some of us men have to go through. I won't even lie, certain times I've got stage fright. Proper fumbled my words.

Quite a few times I have spoken to a girl and she is doing *guy*, acting like she's fly—*bloodyclart* insect. How can a whole me be talking to you and you're giving me rhetoric? So what do I do? I walk off in mid convo. Seven times out of ten the silly trollop comes to speak to me and asks why I walked off? *Why I walked off?* I walked off because you were taking me for Dillon McSweeney, that's why. And then she hits me with more rhetoric: "You should have been more persistent." Per*sist*ent? What the fark? I showered, put on *fine fine* garments, sprayed 'Acqua di gio', I even came to talk to you, and you're asking for per*sist*ence? *I beg:* my name is not Kunle Adepoju.

Seriously, this pride is a joke; it's even got some of you girls who want a relationship, saying that you are 'single by choice'. If the choice is really in your hand, how about you choose to stop being single? I thought you had the power. Go on then. Choose to stop being single right this minute. Or is it the man you want that is rendering you single? If I go to a restaurant where they are serving pork and I don't eat pork, then it isn't a choice, as I don't eat pork. Single by choice? More like single by virtue of rejection. Oh pride, it can proper give some a pillow for comfort. Bit like when a woman says: "Oh, we've been seeing each other for 5 months." Sorry to burst your bubble, but all you've been doing is farking for 5 months. What is seeing each other? Was your vision impaired? Is that what you have settled for, for the past 5 months? . . . Cool.

Pride is a real cockblocker, it really is. Pride will get you acting *stush* when a man wants your number. Pride will get you seeing his call, missing it and calling him the next day. Most men haven't got time for these games. Yes, I will admit there are some assholes in this world but I'm not to blame for the pain that was caused by previous cats.

There is one thing guarding your heart and there is another thing thinking no man is good enough to enter it. That *ish* will leave you out of luck.

Okay, You Swine Of A Man, Get Off Our Case

Like previously stated, don't be scared to ask for help, there is nothing more annoying than a proud woman. We do not like it; it lets us know you're a woman who is pompous and will not back down from an argument. Yes, we have eyes and can see you have a space saver wheel on your car, but can you open your mouth—that you're ever so used to running—and ask for help? We are not your enemy; we are not in a competition. If you see men as your enemy, what is the point in even dating us? Seriously, what is the point? If all you're going to do is give us grief, what is the point?

It's like some women have become snob-like for no reason. Yes, there are some women out there doing their thing and I applaud you—but come on, man. Some of you girls act like your shit smells like beef pattie; this time I know it sizzles off your eyebrows. Then again, some of you take them off to draw them back on with Crayola.

The saddest thing about pride is that it actually could leave you in a dead-end relationship. I know many a woman who are in deadbeat relationships, but won't leave because they don't want to be deemed a failure by their friends and family. They don't want to be seen as being in another broken relationship, so they stay. It's similar to a businessman who won't put the shutters down and call it day because he doesn't want to be deemed a failure, so he keeps pumping money in to the business until the bailiffs come and board it up. Pride is a *bish* that barks at one's ego.

Pride will get you losing the man you want because you didn't want to give off any signs that you liked him. Keep sitting there; good things do not come to those who wait. I don't know who created that idiom, but whoever it was is a liar, man. Keep waiting—please, please, keep waiting. The early bird catches the worm; it's what is leftover that the others get.

Let's drop this pride; it isn't going to help your plight. All this *"doing it like a dude thing"* isn't going to work. Stop trying to compete with us men.

I tell you what most women want: most want the best guy they can find, even though they aren't the best girl *he* can find. They want to *up*grade without caring about someone else *down*grading.

If you aren't bringing anything to the table you will not eat and this goes for MEN too. Don't let your pride consume you. Any man with any gumption will run a mile from a girl who is pompous. These sorts of women tend to find it hard to apologise.

I know there are some bad men out there, but that is the **gamble** of love. I know most men just want to **poke her**, but help us to help you. You have to take some blame on the bad men who *you* have allowed to waltz into your heart. More time it was pride that made you think you could change a scrub into a husband. Ignorance is like putting icing on shit and calling it a cake; *it nah mek it.*

Pride is one thing that I'm working on; the path to a good conscience is dying to self.

Keep playing hard to get and don't be surprised if he *plays*, gets *hard* and then *gets*.

Dear Rob

"It's okay to lose your pride over someone you love, but don't lose someone you love over your pride."—Unknown.

If you're looking for a man to complete you,
you've missed the whole point.

So You're Single By Choice?
How About You Choose To Stop Being Single Then?

"If you aren't happy being single you will never be happy in a relationship. Get your own life and love it first, then share it."

—*Unknown*

Hey, salutations to the single-by-choice crew. Yes, it *is* possible to be single by choice. If you're recovering from a broken heart, for instance; you know, when you're trying to slap yourself together for allowing a man to break into your heart, but you can't call the police to cardiac arrest him because you let him enter in the first place. Then, yes, you can be single by choice. If you're at a stage in your life where you are trying to "find yourself", or you're putting your studies/career at the forefront so you're taking a sabbatical from men, then yes, I agree. However, if you want to be in a relationship, why would you want to be single by choice? Do you want to be alone or do you want to be in a relationship? The two statements cancel each other out. It's like saying you're hungry but you're starving yourself by choice. Are you fasting? Why would you want to starve yourself? Unless the options the waiter is presenting isn't to your taste, then it is the waitress who is rendering you hungry. If you're at a restaurant and he brings out the wrong dish, is it not the waiter who is rendering you hungry for the fact he has not presented you with a choice to dig your teeth into? Is it not the man that you actually want that is rendering you single? Because if the power truly is in your hands, as you claim, how about you choose to stop being alone? I am not single by choice; the woman who has my rib that is eluding me is rendering me single. If the women who cross my path do not tickle my fancy, are they a choice? If you want a pink beetle and I bring you a yellow one, is that choice? It's time for some of you to excise the pride. If you are actively dating and on the dating scene, how can you claim to be single by choice? And even for those who say they don't want to entertain men for now, if Mr Right came along could you really say that you would **cuss a teacher** and **dismiss** because you're taking a **sabbatical** . . .?

Don't allow your pride to keep you single; stop telling yourself that you are single by choice. The more of these affirmations you make about yourself, the more your mind starts to believe it, to the point where you use that phrase as your excuse as to why you are single.

What To Do With My Single Self?

Use this time to better yourself. Being single is not a disability; you don't need to head to the council to go on benefits. Use this as a time to make sure that when you actually meet a man that you're ready. If you're looking for a man to complete you, you're in trouble. If you need a man, you're in trouble. Use this moment to ensure that when Mr Man meets you, you're not left behind because you weren't on par. You can't come around with your short arms and deep pockets; nope, sorry, those days have gone. Cute is out. A woman who can cook and clean is not something that looks impressive on a woman's résumé. Most men can do this for themselves. If that is all you're bringing to the table, you can kindly sit outside—many thanks, amen, cheers. Relationships are all about leverages; who needs who more. Yeah, you may have a nice **bum,** but are you an **ass**et to a man or a liability? When you're in a place in your life and are doing well for yourself, it is highly unlikely that a man will rubbish you, as he knows you don't need him and you can do "all bad" by yourself. When you have to cleave unto the **boxers** of a man, he knows your life is **pants**, so **y front**? You can't act like you're the **shit** when in reality you're just **constipated**. I would say it is important to be able to take care of you before embarking on a relationship; use this time to find "you". Finding "you" may be like a network of paths and hedges designed as a puzzle, but it will amaze you when you find the way. If you don't love yourself, how can you give love to someone else? You can't draw from an empty well. Opportunities are not lost; they are just taken by someone else who was ready and in a better position than you. Luck is being ready for when the opportunity arises. So, yes, being single is not a moment for you to wallow and lick your wounds. Use this as a time to find yourself; a time to better yourself so when he does waltz into your life, he doesn't moonwalk out.

I've Got The Booty *And* The Beauty

Sorry, babes, a lot of men are becoming wiser; the two of those attributes may get him to sleep with you, but to get you out of your singledom . . .? I beg to differ. There are a lot of men who are looking past that. Yes, it's nice to have a girl who has a symmetrical face and has an ass that looks like it's holding her hostage, but that isn't going to hold up my fortress if I fall off—or, G-d forbid, I am in an accident. Your booty and beauty isn't going to be enough. If all you intend to offer a man is what is in between your legs, you may find that is what you may get used for. If you think you can solely get by on looks alone you will be pleasantly surprised how long you may stay single for. If all you can do for a man is look like a trophy—in most cases, a man will not see you as a suitable mate to reproduce with. A woman who can't add anything into a man's life, who can't contribute something, may be subject to what is considered Oyster Card Syndrome (*Touch and Go*).

Some men don't want to feel like they are being used. Don't get me wrong, there are men out there who don't mind this sort of woman who only has her looks and body to offer a man, but a lot of men are opening their eyes and seeing that this sort of woman is of no benefit. If all you're relying on is your looks to get you out of singlehood, you've got another thing coming, my dear friend. As a woman you need to be useful; not only to a man but to yourself. If as a woman all you can offer is sex, don't be surprised if that is what you get used for. A man who has no demonstrable use to a woman tends to get rubbished by women and tends to sit on the bench, forever waiting for some woman who has pity on him to give him a chance. So if you as a woman don't have any demonstrable use to a man, what makes you think you should be plucked out of singlehood?

Listen to Wale's 'Ambitious Girl' Part 1 and 2.

From Work To Home, From Home To Work

Now, how do you intend to break this singledom you're in, if you don't go out? You stay at home on weekends and play with your cat—no, get your mind out the gutter; I'm talking about the pet you bought. That moment when you threw in the towel and thought *fark it*, I'm going to buy a cat to keep me company. That cat is not going to replace the yearning for a man. It's only a temporal fix. Get out there and mingle. Some of you drive to work Monday to Friday, stay in on Saturday, and then go shopping on Sunday. As stated before, it seems that it's been deemed a faux pas for men to chat women up on the street, so where do you intend to meet people? Help me to understand, I am flummoxed. You can't complain and say you no longer want to be single when all you do is sit at home. So many women are opposed to online dating; if you are one of them, how do you plan to meet someone? It's like someone wanting to win the lottery but refusing to play the pound. Yeah, you might be looking for a *mac* but it is highly unlikely he is going to fall into your lap like one. You have to put yourself out there. How will anyone know about a product if it is not marketed? If you're hiding behind the four walls of your house how do you expect people to meet you? If all your friends are in relationships it may be in your best interest to find another set of friends so that you can go out with them.

I saw him first, so let him quench my thirst.

What is it with the "I saw him first" game some of you bra-wearers have adopted? You know what I'm talking about. A guy walks into a club and your friend points him out; now she can claim him. You aren't allowed to talk to him. What is the meaning? How you can you claim a man that you don't even know? To the point that if that guy comes to talk to you and wants to exchange numbers you won't because your friend saw him first. Irrespective of the fact he likes you and not her. I for one don't understand this. Surely your friend should be happy for you that he likes you? Why would she be upset that he fancies you and not her? Let's grow up a bit and excise this nonsense. It's not by force that a man must fancy you; if he doesn't, why can't he talk to your friend? With men, it's totally different. If I fancy a girl and she seems to be more on my mate, I tell him to go and attack. Go get her, go *getta*. If I can't have her, I'd be more than happy if my mate did. You could be missing out some really good potential with this she-saw-him-first thing. If he doesn't like your friend, why can't he get his Tevin Campbell on and talk to you?

Let's say you're out and your friend asks you to go and speak to a guy for her; the dude turns around and says he fancies you—why would you then say: "Oh, my friend likes you, I can't"? If your friend doesn't want you talking to him, and he likes you, that is some serious form of jealousy. Even a bit crazy. How can you claim a man that doesn't even know you, doesn't even fancy you? Your friend should be happy for you. I really don't understand this whole I-can't-talk-to-you-because-my-friend-likes-you.

The Wingman's Best Friend

Are you subconsciously cockblocking yourself? Do you hang around with a bunch of friends that are much more attractive than you? Do you go out with a friend who is clearly much better looking than you? Do you find that when you go out it's always her that gets chatted up to the point where you've got so bitter than when you're out your face is screwed up like to say you were baptised in garlic sauce? No, don't laugh, I'm actually being serious. If you hang around with a bunch of girls who are 8s and you're a minus 17, you may be involuntarily cockblocking yourself. You have now become the wingman's best friend; in fact, you have now taken on the role of bodyguard, where you now cockblock guys from talking to your friend/friends. You're that girl who says "We never came out to talk to any guys, leave us alone; she doesn't want to talk to you". You're that girl who stands there, looking miserable, when your friend is getting chatted up. Just go and learn the offside rule; right now you're goal hanging. Please clear off.

On a serious note, if you're hanging around with a friend who is clearly better looking than you, you may find that you going out is in vain, due to the fact you're not getting chatted up because everyone wants your hot friend. But bear this in mind: you actually may be the enemy hindering your own progress.

All In All

Enjoy your life while being single; you may not own a business but it's important to love your own company. Love spending time with yourself, so that when you find a man you aren't all up in his *ish*. Pick up a class, whether it is a gym class, Kizomba, anything. Pick up a hobby, so that you have a life, so that when you *do* meet a partner he doesn't become your life.

As much as the two of you will come together, you are two individuals. If a man can sense you're the clingy type from the get go, this may put him off. No situation is permanent; even your friends who are in a relationship can become single. Don't feel hard done by. Single is a state that you're in now; there is a season for everything. So yes, use this time to prune yourself. Use it as a time to heal if you need to; take your heart to cobblers and get it attended to. Being single is not a disability; it is important to have the ability to make the best of this situation. Things that you may not be able to do when single, like going on a girl's holiday, do it now. If you're a miserable so-an-so do not, for one second, think that getting into a relationship will change that. You may be pleasantly surprised.

If you're looking for a man to complete you,
you've missed the whole point.

You Want His Heart But It's Your Legs He Wants To Spread Apart

"Sex alleviates tension. Love causes it."

—*Woody Allen*

Women tend to need that emotional intimacy before they put energy into a man; men tend to need that physical intimacy before putting energy into a woman. Oh what a crazy set of species we are. It's finding that balance that seems to plague one another at the beginning; as you can see, we've reached a hurdle. He wants sex first before showing his interest; she wants his heart before she shows interest. This is where a lot of us crash at the beginning. Girl meets guy, she 'respects' her body so has no intention of sleeping with him for a while. Now this guy is most probably thinking: *why is this girl playing games?* The fact she is not *freeing up the naan bread* could read to him that she is not interested, therefore he decides to show less interest in her and transfers his energy where it will be received with open arms. Now it's not all men who will dismiss a woman for taking her time to have sex with him. A lot of men can wait due to the fact that he may be having sex elsewhere anyway, so he can take his time like a sniper waiting to kill his prey—and then attack when need be. And yes, there are guys who can wait for her and won't dip his nugget in another sauce. Those men are there, but they tend to get dismissed as they don't fit the stereotype fly guy. Doesn't fit the mould of what most women look for in a man aesthetically.

The fact that a man may want sex before he puts energy into you is one thing that hinders a lot of women's progress with men. Of course you should only sleep with a man when you're ready; one shouldn't feel pressured into doing so because if *ish* goes titties up you're only going to regret it. So what does one do? I hear the phrase: "If he really likes you he will wait." Well, one could flip that around and say, "If she really likes you she will free it up." Can one really say that if he really likes you he will wait for you when you're ready? One has to remember that some men need that physical intimacy before they decide to show interest in a female; without him sampling the goods, he most probably isn't really that wrapped up in your world. Yeah, he may lust for you but you're not the only girl in this world, and if he meets a girl who is just as cool as you, ticks the boxes like you do, but doesn't make him wait three months to have sex, he might jump ship. I hear you saying: "Then it's his loss." Well, he could also say: "It's her loss." Works both ways.

It's this balance that seems to be causing huge problems, especially for people who subscribe to the notion of 'No sex before marriage'. Now, that may be a hard pill to swallow for many a man; a very hard pill to swallow. I don't know what I'd do if a girl told me that she wasn't going to have sex until her wedding day. I'd die a little inside. *No sex before marriage . . .?* What does she expect me to do with my male member? The craziest thing is that most of these women that subscribe to this *no sex before marriage* thing will be opposed to that man sleeping with someone else. So he likes you—yes, he does—but mammals have an innate desire to want to mate. The whole *no sex before marriage* goes back to the primitive times. I'm sure most of us have watched films like *Robin Hood*, where dads would put their daughters in chastity belts to preserve their virginity. Back in those days, daughters were a commodity. A woman who was a virgin was a valuable asset to her father. A woman who was not a virgin was deemed as a disgrace. Dads literally locked their daughters up. It's from this where *no sex before marriage* practices stemmed from. A virgin was a commercial asset to her father. It was common practice in those times to pay the father of the bride a fee for protecting his daughter's chastity. Women were seen as goods and were sold. Women who were not virgins were not desired for marriage. This paved the way for prostitution; these were the women who were found not to be virgins by the grooms' mothers. Seeing as men wanted to have sex and didn't want to marry non-virgins, some women capitalised on this and decided to sell their body for sex.

Learn something new every day.

Now, you can see where this *no sex before marriage* thing stems from. Women were deemed as property in the primitive times; this was installed into many religious beliefs and then reinforced with the stamp of G-d. So now it's no longer man not wanting sex before marriage, it's G-d. Oh, what a world. Can two people having sex be a sin? Two people who love each other exchanging energy and vibrations be a sin? Or has it been installed in religion as another form of population control?

I understand the double standard when it comes to sex. Women tend to get labelled hos and men get labelled players. I know it's crazy. But to be fair most men will only label you a ho if you sleep with them on the same night you meet them; or if you sleep with them on the first date. Also, if you get shared around the group like pass the parcel, once again you may be seen as loose. If you sleep with more than one guy on your menstrual cycle then, yes, once again you will be judged to be a ho. There was this one girl I was sleeping with who I was actually contemplating taking serious, but lo and behold she was sleeping with my mate at the same time. She never knew that we knew each other. Now this girl ended up sleeping with both of us within twenty-four hours. G-d forbid she got pregnant; she would be none the wiser who the dad is. It's these kinds of things that get females labelled as a ho. We are not the same species, so we are not governed by the same stigma.

He wants sex but you want him to wait. The funniest thing is that most of the time some of you women are actually gagging for it (excuse the pun) but just decide to keep him waiting. Well, unfortunately, dating seems to have become a form of modern day prostitution. Yes, I said it. Some females will withhold the sex from a man until she feels he has paid enough. A lot of men have realised this; that for some women, they expect a man to make vagin payments. This means he's taken you out on three dates, spent let's say £200 in total—as far as he is concerned he's made the payments. For instance, let's say I've taken you out, we've got to know each other (whatever getting to know each other means), and now I want to sample my purchase; in many a man's head one is thinking to themselves how many more dates: *how much more money will I have to spend before I can get to the cat?* Yes, I appreciate it's not all women that need money spent on them before one can have sex, but, with the men and women I have asked, it seems to be the case for some.

Okay, so he has spent time and money on dating you and still no reward. He is more than likely pissed. *Man needs to stroke the cat, man needs to stroke Sheba. What is the meaning?* Now, a lot of men can and will continue dating you till they get the cat. But if they are sleeping with someone else while dating you that means the basis of your relationship was built on a foundation of him sleeping with someone else. This means in his mind, he is used to sleeping with other women while with you. This can cause huge problems. How something as natural as sex can cause so many issues—it's crazy.

This abstinence from sex will forever cause problems between some men and some women, as *she* wants his heart first and *he* wants the cat first. And even when she may have his heart, she may not want to give up the sex until marriage. Would one really want to marry someone without knowing whether they are sexually compatible with each other? If this is the partner you intend on settling down with for 'life', would it not make sense to know whether or not the dude could blow you up like the World Trade Centre?

Well, Houston, we don't have a problem as he can't even lift off. If you're a virgin I can understand why you would want to preserve your virginity and I fully respect that. But if you *aren't* one—ermmmmm, yeah, okay.

Even in the primitive times there was something which they called trial marriages. It was at this point where a man and woman would have sex and try and see if she could conceive. If she couldn't, the marriage would be annulled. What would you do if you married someone and they were infertile? What would you do if you married a man and he was wack in bed? Would you really be happy with using your vibrator for the rest of your life? Obviously, if you're a virgin you most probably won't know the difference between good sex and bad sex—unless your friends ask you if your vagin has ever involuntarily contracted six-plus times, or if they ask you if you have ever been short for breath when having sex like to say you were having an asthma attack. Sexual compatibility is important in a relationship. Very, *very* important.

What to do? What to do? Either way it's your body, but just bear in mind many a man will lose interest in you if you decide to starve your cat from good loving. The funniest thing about it is that if you're a virgin, he most likely would wait until the wedding day—but most of you aren't. (I'm an asshole, I know.)

This is one situation/scenario where I don't feel a compromise can even be met without one feeling hard done by (excuse the pun). If you refuse to give him sex, he may get it from somewhere else which I doubt you will be happy with. So how does one overcome this hurdle? I don't even know myself. I guess one will just have to find someone who is willing to wait or willing to lie to you that they aren't sleeping with anybody else. Happy days.

If you're looking for a man to complete you,
you've missed the whole point.

If I Sleep With Him, Will He Respect Me In The Morning?

"Sex always has consequences. When Hitler's mother spread her legs that night, she effectively cancelled out the spreading of fifteen to twenty million other pairs of legs."

—George Carlin

Dear Rob, The Cat's Purring, Sheba Is Crying Out For Him

Looking at a man and getting cold shivers is commonplace; it's what a fine boy with no pimples can do to you.

The question is: what to do with this lasciviousness? Well, well, well, give him the cat, *innit*. I kid, I kid. Before even sleeping with a man, you have to ask yourself one thing: "Will we be able to stand if I fell pregnant for him? Does he have the resources to maintain a family?"

YOU SEE THAT GUY YOU'RE SLEEPING WITH, CAN HE AFFORD TO HAVE KIDS? IF NOT, WHY ARE YOU SLEEPING WITH HIM?

Yes, Sheba may be yearning for him; yes, the butterflies may be swirling in your stomach, but seriously—can the dude that is making Sheba salivate raise a family if you were to get pregnant? Chomp on that for a hot Nigerian minute.

Before we even address the point of "Will he respect me in the morning?" ask yourself another question: are you respecting your womb? Are you aware that four out of ten pregnancies are unplanned? Based on a survey carried out on three thousand women on evriwoman.co.uk. She's calling him a *pussio* and he's calling her *derk head*—oh the irony. And for no minute am I putting the blame on women, but as history has proved a man can do an **Osama Bin Hiding**, blow your belly up and leave you with the **aftermath** and there will be nothing **Dr. Dre** can do it about it. He may buy you some **M&Ms** to sweet you up.

Okay, Rob, Everything Seems In Cheque, Can I Let Him Make A Deposit Into My Account?

Never ever sleep with a man based on what he has told you; like **50 cent**, **many men** are salesmen. They will pitch you, promise you the world and then give you an atlas. Well, hey, he did as he promised.

I come to you in the name of Iqbal Jahasaphat of the seven seas and treacherous waters, never ever sleep with a man on his words, never ever.

Sleep with a man on your onus. Sleep with him when you feel comfortable in doing so. Some men have a silver tongue, and they won't even use it to go down on you. Certain men will tell you they love you, just to get a slice of the cake. Some men will tell you that they will blow you up in the bedroom, this time they're nothing more than a bomb threat. The discipline some men put into trapping Sheba is ridiculous; if they put the same zeal into their careers they wouldn't have to chase the cat and end up with it getting stuck up a tree.

If you sleep with a man on what he has said to you, you may end up falling, and if he hasn't got a parachute for you, what next? The first thing on most (not all) men's minds when they see a fine specimen of a *wombman's* venturing across the abyss on a fine summers day is SEX, SEX, SEX. From the moment some men get your number they are writing their contingency plan; their thesis on how they will attack the cat. They are forming their **rap**, so that they can get the **beat** and not be left with an **accapella**. In order to get the cat, some men have to make an impression, while with others their aura speaks volumes. A man who has to sing a Donnel Jones rendition to capture Sheba is trying to make an impression. The truth does not need a mouthpiece to speak for it.

Before you trip, slip and find his fingers on your clit, ask yourself: "What do I want from this?" Is it just sex or do I actually want him as my man? This is simply for you; it has nothing to do with the man. If a man's sole intention is to **just blaze** and make you a **beat**, whatever you have conjured up in your head is irrelevant. This is to get your own mind into perspective as to whether you intend to affix your emotions or not. This is the ultimate decider, I believe, on whether you get hurt or not. Sex is a serious *ting* when a man knows how to reach the cervix. *"Dick power be no joke, oh."* When a man can leave your left leg shaking and leave your kitty cat throbbing the next day for some more action—*"it be no small ting."* Good dick will get you hooked like a crack fiend.

Certain men will not care whether you can swim or not, they will feel no way drowning you with their backstroke. As previously stated, only free up the cat when you feel comfortable. I will let you into a secret: if you have already told a man he is not getting the cat and he somehow twangs you into getting it, it will put you at a disadvantage as he now knows that you can be coerced into having sex, which may mean that some next man could also do the same. Stay strong. If you've told him no—no is no. Don't deceive yourself by letting him kiss you; don't let him get a stroke of the *fanjita*. It's better you stick to your guns than giving him the satisfaction that he was able to wiggle his worm into your apple.

Can I Hit It In The Morning? No C-Brown But Will You Respect Me?

I once read a book by a man who said that women should implement a ninety-day rule before she has sex with a new partner. In other words, a woman should make a man wait three months before allowing him to make a deposit in her princess purse. Now, what I would like to know is: what does that prove? Is this supposed to make a man respect you more? Well, I beg to differ. If you're a bit of a loose goose and he does his HPI check on you, you making him wait one year doesn't make a difference. Sorry there aren't any born again virgins round here, mate. If the three months is to see whether he is interested in you, or to see whether he has self-control, I ask you one question: are you going to smell his fingers and his penis every time he walks through the door? When some men chat up women they are already tucking someone in on the side, they are already hitting their balls into the back of the net. So while some men are waiting to get the cat, they are more than likely stroking someone else's in the meantime; you making him wait means Nathan; it doesn't prove he is a gentleman. I know many a man who have taken a girl on a date, dropped her home and then drove to Sandra's to give her the pipe. When a man meets a girl, more time he knows what his intentions are for her. Men are not indecisive by nature. The reason you remained a link wasn't a mistake. It's your character that matters. Put it this way: if your HPI check comes back with discrepancies, you making me wait means *nada*. All I would say to you is that if you want to encourage a man to take you seriously, avoid sleeping with him on the first night, but even in doing this, if your character is good, he can and may hold onto you.

The respect doesn't only come from the act of sex; it comes from your background check. If a man knows you're a bit easy—meaning you sleep with more than one man on the same cycle, no pushbike—or you get treated like *pass the parcel,* as in you've slept with numerous men in the same camp/scene, then, as I've said, you making him wait is irrelevant. Yes, there are men out there who will wife these girls; the same way there are men out there who will buy a girl flowers, have sex and never be seen again.

You can make a man wait five weeks for the sex, but remember: women tend to find it hard to go back financially when it comes to dating and men tend to find it hard to go back sexually. If the sex is wack, you making him wait may leave you at a disadvantage because now you've grown feelings for dude and he no longer wants to play with kitty. Just a bit of food for thought.

That myth that the longer you make a man wait the more he will respect you is nonsense as far as I am concerned. There are men in this world who may say the duration matters, but that is most probably because they've always had to wait—and that's probably because women most probably didn't find them sexually attractive, so it was their personality that grew on them, no Mark Morrison.

Men shouldn't confuse the two. A woman making you wait doesn't necessarily mean that she is a good girl; she may simply not fancy you like that. Just remember: the same girl that you treat nice, next man have just run through. For every pretty girl back on the market, just remember someone was tired of shagging her; sounds harsh, but it's reality. If I would give any advice on whether he would respect you in the morning I would say it boils down to the man, as not every man is the same. The best thing to do is to avoid sleeping with a man on the first night if you actually see any potential in him. If it's just sex you require, *pffftt,* go ahead, do your thing, whatever puts a jam in your doughnut. As I have continuously stressed it's your character and HPI check that will determine whether a man will respect you. In my experience and talking with the many dogs I have had the pleasure of mingling with, this is what has become a reality.

With all the above said, bear this in mind, there's something some of us men call 'The Chat'. 'The Chat' is the lengthy conversation you have with a woman which opens the floodgates; the chat that basically seals the beat. That chat that when you hang up you actually don't realise you were talking for that long. It's the moment when, even you as a female are like: *Hmmm, I like this guy's flavour.*

Think back to the conversations that you have had with a guy that put you at ease; that time where you put your **mitts** down and finally dropped your **guard** and decided that you want to see what's in his **boxers**. It's 'The Chat' that is needed to give a guy confidence that you've actually attempted to get to know him. You can't expect a guy to respect you when you are sleeping with him and you don't even know what he does for a living or where he lives, etc. There are some fundamentals that you as a woman should know about a man before you open **sesame** and let him put his **big bird** in your play centre. Well, **Julia knows best**—man, I'm giving away too much **here** (bet that went over your head). You've got to have 'that conversation'; don't forget 'that conversation'. Very important.

In Closing

Let me pose a question: errmmm, where has getting to know someone actually got us? Can we ever really get to know someone? Do people not change? What does getting to know someone mean? After you know his name, age, what he does for a living, whether he has kids, whether he is packing (no vacation)—after you've known the fundamentals, what really is there left to know? We as men can play 'Perfect Paul' and take you on strolls down the Damascus Road prior to getting the cat, but it's after then that you may realise things aren't always **black** and **white,** and then you'll see his true **colours**.

It's in a human's disposition to act in a way that will favour them at the beginning. Hence, many a man will get the job and then get sacked—why is that? Yes, there are some people who are genuine, but that you will never know until you take the risk. Time is the best answer.

Sleep with a man on your onus not on what he has said to you. Making a man wait three months doesn't mean *ish*; that's if you're using this as method to gauge whether he can curb his sex urge. I am bold enough to say that most men are beating something on the side and I don't mean a talking drum, okay Fella (bet you missed the pun there). If you want to get to know a guy before sleeping with him by all means do so to satisfy YOURSELF. Yes, I said YOURSELF. If a man's intention is to do uninsured driver on you and hit and run, he will.

If you're looking for a man to complete you,
you've missed the whole point.

Why Won't He Make Me Wifey? I'm Tired Of This *Shet*

"The lion does not turn around when a small dog barks."
—African Proverb

What Is It, Dear Rob, That Makes A Man Think She Isn't Ms Right But Ms Right Now?

I will start by saying 99.9% of the time a man knows whether he intends to take you seriously or whether you are going to be a link. It's not a fluke that you were kept hanging around like a pair of double f's with no bra for months on end. He had no intention of making you wife. As I have said before men are not indecisive by nature. If you've been long stroking and deep poking with a man for more than three months and he is *uhmmmming* and *arrrrghhiiinnnng*, most circumstances you are going to be a link.

If he is dedicating time to you in that three months and the time you spend together is intense, it is enough time in most circumstances for him to determine what he wants to do with you.

A woman who can keep a home, cook, and has the Scheherazade Effect (I will elaborate on this further on) will always be a keep-her. When a man has a woman who can sex good but the food is wacko and the house is not a home, be aware that he may have a side chick AKA Sweetcorn who is filling the gap. Hence, he wasn't hungry.

Women Who Rave A Lot

This for many men is a huge turn off; a very huge turn off. A woman who is on the scene who is 'everybody's' friend in most cases will never be taken seriously.

No man wants a woman who raves all the time; no man wants a commercial chick. This is one thing that is rendering you nothing more than a beat. When you're that girl who is in every photographer's album, it is not a good look.

A woman who raves a lot is an instant no-no. This will automatically put you in the friend box; don't worry, feel free to network in there, you aren't alone.

The Way She Markets Herself

You are the marketing force that drives your campaign. The way you dress is so important, *so* important, and it seems like a lot of you women haven't grasped this. The manner in which some of you dress when going out is shocking, seriously shocking.

You don't need to expose your whole body to be sexy. A bit of decorum is oh-so needed. A man looking at a woman with her tits and legs out of the door like an Avon catalogue is thinking one thing: SEX SEX SEX. He is not thinking 'wifey'.

A lot of you girls take pictures of yourselves in your underwear and then post them on Facebook. These sorts of things are nothing short of a cry for sexual admiration. You put the pictures up and then you get the swine clicking 'like' on them and making asinine comments. In most cases these girls never have as many comments on their pictures when they are fully clothed.

The manner in which you dress speaks volumes and if it's provocative it will be hard for a man to turn down his desires. We tend to assess what the book is about before we open it up. Telling a man to respect you whilst dressing like you're selling is oxymoronic. It makes no sense.

Why as a woman would you want men ogling over your body? Is the reason you get chatted up more than your friend because you're perceived as the apple on the floor? Ladies, you have to take some responsibility when it comes to this. If a man came to talk to you with his jeans at his knees, walking like he has a leg shorter than the other, with a hood on his head, I'm quite sure you would be apprehensive. Why is that? It's a rhetorical question; you need not answer as you already know why. The manner which you present yourself speaks volumes.

I can't emphasise this enough; show that you respect yourself in the way you dress and you may see a different sort of man approaching you. As they say, you are what you attract. You may not be a loose goose but you sure are dressing like one. When a man is looking for a woman to take home or to put his male member in; if it's just sex he wants he is more than likely going to go for what he deems as the easy target, and if you're dressed in a ho-like manner, or present yourself in one, he will deal with you accordingly.

As a lady you can't wear a tight dress that looks like it was tattooed on your skin and not expect a man to look at you as a sexual object.

Her Character

This here is so crucial. I asked a few of the lads what was the deciding factor in what made you want to settle with your missus and here are a few of the statements they made:

"In the time I was wooing her, trying to get the ass, I got to know her and realised she kept me smiling." Highlighting the words 'kept me smiling'. Some of you girls are just miserable sods. I keep telling women the longer you stay in a broken relationship the worse you make it for you and your new partner.

A woman with a cheerful disposition will always be wanted around. A woman whose face looks clenched like a fist will not.

Another quote: "She was thoughtful, helpful and had initiative." I have to applaud that; both my exes had the exact same qualities.

Thoughtful and helpful; a woman who actually wants to help, that doesn't have to be coerced or cajoled. You're on the phone to a man and he says he might go to Birmingham tomorrow but doesn't know the train times. A thoughtful, helpful woman with initiative will put on the laptop and find out times and where he can get the train from. I don't think you understand how much points you get for that. When a man and woman can work in unison there is no greater partnership, none.

Your demeanour is so crucial; being a pleasant woman will get you far with a man. One thing you lovely ladies need to understand is that it's not everything you need to argue about. A nagging woman will not make wifey; she will not. I left home six years-plus, I don't need a woman nagging me, thank you very much, amen. *He left the toilet seat up.* "So? There are kids dying in third world countries; next argument." Just put the seat down; it's not that big a deal.

A man wants a woman he can feel free around, a woman he can chill with. It is imperative that there is a common interest between the two of you.

If the man you are interested in likes football, go and read up about it. It shows you care; you will gain 10000000000000000000000 (sorry, got carried away with the zeros) points by simply understanding the offside rule and knowing what is going on in the football world.

If the man you are interested in likes computer games, the simple fact that you and him play together forms a common interest.

If all you two have in common is sex, then sex is what it will be. A common interest between the two of you is crucial. Most men are sleeping with more than one woman, and I'm not saying it is a competition but you need to stick out like nipples on a cold day.

One of my exes I met in the gym, so we used to go to the gym together and that was our common ground. So at times we would train together.

I knew from the get-go I wanted her to be my girl but what sealed the deal was the fact she didn't mind coming out with me when I was out making money.

Credit Checks

It's at this hurdle I would say seventy percent of you fail, which is why you don't reach *wifey* status. The world is a very small place. You can't get away with *ish*. If you have been a slag in your past, it will creep up on you. When many a man wants to take a girl seriously, they will run a HPI.

He wants to make sure you are not on finance, ensure your mileage hasn't been tampered with, and verify that you haven't been written off. It's a shame really because it's us guys who make women slags, coupled with some women's naivety.

I keep telling girls who like to have sex that the travel card extends past zone 4. Travel off ends. You can't keep sleeping with guys in the same camp, you can't. News spreads. As much as you are a good sport, in most instances you won't make wifey (but if you're really lucky you might be able to retrieve Dillon from the friend zone).

If a man asks you how many men you have slept with—if it is over ten: lie lie lie, lie like your mattress depends on it. Even if he has told you that he has slept with eighty-five, do not think that gives you the right to tell him fourteen. You will be handed your p45 *noicely*. I implore you, *muddatuckking* lie.

Nobody wants to think of your previous notches and then envisage the whole of the Arsenal football team; it's not a good look.

Suicidal Moves On Social Networks And Extra Curricular Activities

The kind of things some of you girls say on social networks is enough to call you Ramaman (suicide bombers). Even if you were drunk, why do you feel the need to tell the whole of Twitter? It is not something commendable in a man's eyes. No man is going to want his missus to be coming home smashed out of her head. If my missus came home drunk, I would lock her in the toilet; maybe she can use that time to sync back decorum and etiquette together. As far as I am concerned, it is not lady like. These things will keep you as a link.

Posting stupid videos and pictures of you on the Internet is not needed; as much as you may see it as fun, it is suicidal. Videos of you booty shaking et al, may be fun to you but to many a man it may be a deal breaker.

Only G-d knows why women do this and then complain they can't find a good man. Shit attracts flies.

I was seeing a girl in 2010 and she was hot, blah blah blah, then she disclosed to me that she does music videos. I then saw a calendar she was in. I said "hell to the mf no" to that. So one day I will go to my mate's house and see him bashing with the lotion over a picture of my chick . . .? *G-d forbid, badting*. I handed her, her p45.

Damn, she was good to me . . .

Scheherazade Effect

This was first highlighted by a cognitive psychologist called Geoffrey Miller. It refers to the ploy that women used in the primitive times to keep a man. This refers to skills and charm women had: their conversational skills; the manner in which she would interact with a man. As I have stated earlier, you need to have a common interest with a man. If it's just sex, when he is finished with you, he may hand you your p45. The Scheherazade Effect is in reference to the film called Arabian Nights. The sultan would have women around him for a while, use them for sex, and when he was done with them would have them executed. Sad, I know. But one day he came across Scheherazade. A woman who was good at storytelling; she had a way of stimulating him mentally. *Stimulate* him physically and you might have him for the night; *stimulate* him mentally and you might have him for life. Even though she was to be beheaded after spending the night, he kept her around and ended up having kids with her. Being able to connect with a man is important. Being able to hold a conversation with him that interests him is important. You see the man you're dating, or with now, do you have the Scheherazade Effect on him? It's this that will separate you from the rest. Find out what interests him and go and research that field; find out about the current affairs. Don't let another *bish* sit on your throne.

In Closing

Each and every man will have his little tick list of things he refuses to accept in a woman. For some, it's women with weave. Sure, that man will sleep with her, but she will never be Ms Right; she will be Ms Right Now. Don't for one second think that a man sleeping with you means he likes you. You will be pleasantly embarrassed.

For some men, it's kids. Some men refuse to date women with kids, so that could be his gripe. The fact that you move with loose gooses is another reason why he may say "hell no, I can't take you serious". The fact that you are broke and not showing any drive to get out of that situation could be another reason. If you are not bringing anything to the table you will not eat. When I was on my face back in 05, I left girls the hell alone.

The ultimate killer could be the simple fact that you know too much road man. This here is an instant turn off. Going through your pictures and seeing you with 'killermanwithoneshotifimissstabhim' is not going to get you any points, it is not. Take those pictures down. The social network has ruined it for a lot of you girls.

As stated earlier your character is crucial. With any man you are dating, you have to find a common ground so one can put a vocal to the track and make a beautiful ensemble. If not you will be nothing more than a beat.

You lovely ladies have to learn to give things in rations. You can't be cooking, cleaning, polishing the TV and him, and bringing him lunch as a link. If you are doing all of that as a link, why should he upgrade you? Show him you can cook and then *pause*. Show him you can suck a mean dick and then *pause*. Show him the levels and then halt. Some of you are doing way too much. Show him the levels and then let him know if he wants more of this, he knows what he needs to do.

Needless to say if your sex is wack, you will never make wifey. In fact, these girls get lost like a set of keys . . . But, hey, G-d is good and Chambord is *tasty*. Most men can't go back sexually and most women can't go back financially, it's just what it is.

If you're looking for a man to complete you,
you've missed the whole point.

Beauty Is YOU, Every Other Opinion Is Subjective

"Everything has beauty, but not everyone sees it."
—*Confucius*

Let me start off by saying beauty is subjective, so why would you expect every *mofo* to find you attractive? Beauty is YOU. Yes, beauty is you, you are beauty, you are cynosure; one of a kind. No one on the face of this earth has the same fingerprint as you. Ask **Andre 3000,** you are the **prototype**. But what is it that gets a vain man's blood pumping from his heart to his pencil and gets him to think hubba-hubba?

As you should be aware, men are visual creatures. Men and women vary in amygdala response to visual sexual stimuli. Men, in general, are more concerned and receptive to visually sexually arousing stimuli than women. A man may be broke but he will have enough to pay attention to your exterior. It's not your personality that first draws us to you—no, it is not. We cannot see your personality. As much as one can paint an idea of how one may be from the way one dresses, one cannot determine what their personality is like until one converses with them.

Have You Fallen Out With Your Face? Is That Why You Always Want To Make Up?

Are you and your face on good terms? The day women stop putting graffiti on their face is the day us men will approach you with the truth. We're both lying to each other. Bat wings for eyelashes, blond weave on dark skin women, got them looking like Mufasa. Come on, ladies, are you really trying to live up to the media hype? If you keep trying to follow the media's interpretation of beauty you're going to end up looking like Li'l Kim: a confused question. Truth be told, the vast majority of men abhor makeup, we sure do. Mascara and some lipstick/lip gloss is cool. But why would you erase your eyebrows only to then take colouring utensils from a child's pencil case and draw them back on? You are beautiful. Yes, YOU that are reading. You are beautiful. No matter how much makeup and enhancements one wears, your eyes cannot hide your insecurities. There is nothing wrong in wearing makeup, but when you can't leave your house without wearing some, that is when you have to look inside yourself and ask a few questions. The people that some of you are trying to emulate do not look like they do on TV. It is makeup and a lot of photo shopping. No one who walks this earth's surface is perfect. Why would you want to keep up with Kim Kar-dash-her-in-a-bin? Are you aware of how much surgery she has undergone? These women, who some of you have put on a pedestal, have gone under the knife to look the way they look. There is nothing more off putting than a woman drowned in makeup. Come as you are, so we can accept you for who you are. We are not generally pleased by the fake. Confidence is sexy. Learn to love you. How can you give love if you don't love yourself? You can't draw from an empty well. From the many men I have asked, they say they do not like a face drenched in makeup; some put up with it but they categorically do not like it.

Be happy with who you are. All a whole heap of makeup indicates to many a man is that one may be insecure, and an insecure woman is a nightmare for a man, because in most cases she will always need affirming about her looks.

A Woman With A Body Will Make A £4.99 Dress Look Like A Million Dollars

Your body makes a huge difference, it sure does—especially if you're obese. I've seen women with faces that are **Precious,** but with a banging body, get hounded by men. When asking men about whether they would prefer a woman with an 8-face but a 6-body or a woman with a 6-face but 8-body, the majority preferred the latter. Sexiness and attractiveness are two different things. A woman may be attractive, but it is her body that will make her sexy. Body shape is important. If the only six packs your body is use to is Premium or Remi, get to the gym and put your fitness first.

It doesn't take a rocket scientist to know that any sane man loves a woman with a nice body—oh, we sure do. It not only looks pleasing to the eye, it also indicates that you like to look after your body. It shows that you don't only look after your temple from the neck up. So many women spend hours on their head, but seem to neglect the rest of their body. Hey you, yes you, get your ass in the gym.

Women with a WHR (waist to hip ratio) of 0.7—indicating a waist significantly narrower than the hips—are most desirable to men. In my own findings of asking men what they deemed attractive, most of them found women with wider hips more attractive. We as men love curves. Psychologist Devendra Singh of the University of Texas studied people's waist-to-hip ratio (WHR). In an analysis of hourglass figures of Playboy models and Miss America contestants, it showed that the majority of these women boast a WHR of 0.7 or lower. The hourglass figure, also known as the Coca Cola bottle shape, is most desired by men. It subconsciously indicates whether you will be a good vessel to bear children. Crazy, I know, but the hips don't lie, ask Shakira.

Where fat is placed on the body is determined by sex hormones; testosterone in men and oestrogen in women. If a woman produces the proper amount and mixture of oestrogen, then her WHR will naturally fall into the looked-for range.

Your diet, what you eat, will also play a part in this; a lot of people seem to mistake what a sea food diet is—and see food and decide to eat. You can near enough eat what you want as long as you exercise. How many of you exercise? When is the last time you went to the gym? I see a lot of women in the gym with a full face of makeup on; if you aren't sweating, you aren't losing weight. Why do you think when boxers/fighters need to cut weight for a big fight they sit in the sauna? They do so, so they can perspire. Your body is your temple; you've got to look after it.

Also, in my asking of men what they found attractive, I can tell you that most men found women with broad shoulders unattractive. I guess some of you have them from all those years of gold digging.

It is said that people in the ideal hip-ratio range, regardless of weight, are less susceptible to disease such as cardiovascular disorders, cancer, and diabetes. Studies have shown that women in this range also have less difficulty conceiving.

So, as you can see, your body plays a huge factor in a man approaching you and looking at you as a woman to bear his offspring.

I May Not Have A Bum, Butt Why Should That Make Him Back Off?

"I love big butts and I cannot lie"—words from Sir Mix A Lot. This song emphasised the love that so many men have for a woman with an ass that looks like it's holding her hostage. Oh, we love a noice ass. Yummy. It's funny how the same thing that Europeans ridiculed Sara Baartman for having, so many are craving now.

Even our closest relatives in the animal kingdom (primates) have an infatuation with a female's bottom. They hold a severe attraction for it. Amongst primates, a female's bottom protrudes and can change colour to indicate they are ready for mating. Female humans are the only primates with permanently enlarged derrieres. Humans and bonobos are also the only primates that mate face to face (missionary). In other primate species, males approach females from the back, check to make sure her buttocks are swollen and have turned red, then pounce and go for the kill. Therein lies the attraction for males and a woman's derriere. We just love a nice peachy ass. It boils down to more than simply one's preference. A woman's back luggage also has two very important purposes: it stores fat for breastfeeding and acts as an emergency food storage in lean times, similar to a camel's hump.

For those whose ass resembles a Nando's drink (bottomless) all is not lost. The Gluteus Maximus is a muscle—so what does that mean? It means it can be worked on. The same way other muscles on the body can be worked on. Squats, dead lifts and lunges are three good exercises to get your back-off looking segsee. Remember, it is a muscle, the more you work it, the bigger it will get. Don't be disheartened; get a personal trainer and get him/her to put you through your paces.

Might I add, as you should already know, wearing high-heeled shoes makes a woman arch her back, push out her buttocks, and makes her wiggle when she walks, which habitually draws male attention. We just love the back-off.

(Side note: what was the big who-ha about Pippa Middleton's ass? Maybe I missed something—pun intended—but as you can see her bum made an ass of her sister and stole the show.)

A nice bit of doggy won't do it any harm. The vibrations, too, can get one's ass in shape.

A woman with a bum unequivocally makes a big difference, I can tell you that for free.

"She got an ass that'll swallow up a G-string / and up top, uh, two bee stings"—Kanye West.

I'm A Breast Man But I Rate Asses

Don't get excited, those aren't my words. They are the words of a UK rapper. How could you think they were? How dare you? I am not a breast man; however, there are men who are. So for those of you who don't have an ass that would make a set of French knickers look like a thong, all is not lost. You have the next best thing: breasts.

Apart from producing milk to breastfeed (how milk even comes out of those things beats me), the breasts' main purpose is sexual signalling—nothing more, nothing less. It in some way mimics a woman's derriere; a remnant from the days that humans use to walk on all fours. If a monkey walked up to you on two legs it wouldn't be possible to tell whether it was male or female. It is said that breasts evolved as a mimic of the female rear. Tests have been done with pictures showing a woman's cleavage and bum crack and most men couldn't differentiate between the two.

Yeah, some men *do* like breasts. I couldn't care less for breasts, just have a nice old set of nipples the size of a fingertip and I'm game. But, hey, that's just me. In my findings, I found that most men preferred bum over breasts. But if you haven't got a bum, breasts will suffice. If you haven't got either . . . pause. I will have to look at your passport just to confirm gender. I kid, I kid.

Ultimately, as a woman, there is going to be something on your body which you can use to lure a man in—whether it is your lips, your eyes, your calves. Yes, a lot of men have a thing for women with calf muscles. Learn to work with what you've got. If you've got knuckle-breast, why would you wear a boob tube? What boobs do you have to tube? If you've got flat batty syndrome, wearing leggings may further draw attention to what you don't have. Everyone has their USP—what is yours? Figure what it is and use it to your advantage.

There are three main things that a man will check for when looking at a woman: her face, bum and breasts. But please, remember that beauty is subjective. What a man likes is relative to him; one man's poison is another man's Chambord.

Silent . . . But Your Body Language Speaks A Thousand Words

The way you carry yourself plays a huge part in whether a man will approach you or not. Do you walk around with your face clenched like a fist? Do you look approachable? If you were a man, do you think a man would approach you with the countenance which you portray?

With all that has been said in this chapter, a woman doesn't necessarily have to be beautiful to attract a man. Yes, beauty/curves certainly will give her an initial edge over her rivals. But all she really needs to do is display signs that she could be available; hence, some women who are not necessarily symmetrical in the face have a lot of male compadres. You can be as hot as four black males in a tinted black Golf driving through Downing Street, but if you act like your shit smells like beef pattie, men may shun you. A lot of you ladies who are single act like you aren't. Funniest thing, it seems like the women who are in relationships seem to be more sociable and friendly.

No matter how great your body may be, no matter how great your face may look, you need to show signs of availability. No, you haven't got to walk around like you've got a Chelsea smiley, no. Just show that you aren't a wedgie and that you don't have your head stuck up your ass.

You don't have to be the best looking woman in the club or in your bunch; obviously, being good-looking and having an ass helps, but also looking pleasant is important. I go out at times and I see women in clubs with their face push up like someone's pasted excrement on their top lip. Yes, I understand that some men are like hound dogs and see raves as a meat market, but with your face like that, you are painting a bad picture of yourself literally.

Adjust that screwed up face of yours; let us know that this beauty isn't going to come with attitude. So, yes, relax, let down your hair. If your bra is too tight, try wearing one that isn't wired, or go to your local bra shop and get measured. You women call the shots. You have to throw the bait and get us hooked. Ever gone fishing? The fisherman doesn't throw in bait that *he* likes, no. He throws in bait that the fish will like. Oh, might I add, the vast majority of us abhor weave, just putting it out there. For those who have alopecia or illnesses, I understand. For those who haven't, why are you wearing another woman's hair on your head, covering your crown with another woman's crown? Just imagine if we started wearing fake beards and moustaches; you'd think we were odd. It's a bit cheeky for a woman who stunts with horse hair, to have a problem with a guy stunting in a rental. You have horse hair he has horse power.

Well, hey, it's your body, but I'm just letting you know most of us do not like it. Especially when we're trying to get intimate and we go for your hair—I mean, weave—and you move our hands away, grrrrrr. Some of y'all haven't seen your head top since 2000; weave after weave after weave after weave. I feel for that girl in India who is being chased by a Lion and three hyenas in the jungle, just so that her hair can be chopped off to beautify another woman. And yes, I am aware there are a minority of women who cut their hair off for religious purposes.

Anywho, don't forget squats, dead lifts and lunges . . . and if all else fails, you can get some butt pads. Don't even think of it.

If you're looking for a man to complete you,
you've missed the whole point.

Mr Drug Dealer VS Mr Just Getting By—Who 'Ticks' The Most 'Boxes'?

"If a man has been his mother's undisputed darling he retains throughout life the triumphant feeling, the confidence in success, which not seldom brings actual success along with it."
—Sigmund Freud

Like a girl doing **down**, I have heard this matter **arise** many a times (call me Kenyan, *man a long distance Stulla*). Would you rather date Mr 'Illegal' over Mr 'Just Getting By'?

I Know You Can't Dance, Dear Rob, But Break It Down For Us

Now, let me start by saying that some of the men who are self-employed are doing things that can land them in jail, whether it be evading taxes (Hi, Wesley Snipes—the way he got his 'don't forget you're black' wakeup call is a *madness*. "Don't think because we have allowed you to chill with us and make dough, you can avoid taxes like us." You forgot about OJ, you forget about MJ, you forgot about Chuck Berry, you forgot about James Brown. Sorry, Wesley, we just had to remind ya." "Hey Spike, I thought you said 'Jungle fever' would save me forever?" "It would have but you acted in 'White Men Can't Jump'.")

Now, someone would have said: "Wesley Snipes isn't a drug dealer; isn't a fraudster," but hey, he was robbing the state of their money—and, like me having a threesome, they sure *came* for him.

There are men out there who are working on other people's NI numbers; there are many things people do that can land them in jail.

Who are the two richest sets of people in this world? One owns the Federal Reserve and one owns a vast amount of oil. How did they acquire so much wealth? Slavery. Not saying that all their money came from there, but five-hundred odd years must have contributed a hell of a load.

A lot of focus seems to be put on the Caucasians when it comes to slavery, but it was simply commerce for them. Not that I condone their treatment, but they were sold a commodity by the Jews and the Arabs and they used the product as they wished. Read up on the 'Curse Of Ham'—it will explain a lot.

To my point, some of the people you see who *run* businesses and who have money, more than likely arrived at it in a dodgy way, bar the ones who got a hand out. Yes, there are the select few who may have got a loan out, but there are also the set of people who have *washed* their money.

I have come across a few girls who take drugs but say they won't date a drug dealer. What kind of nonsensical nonsense is that? You're happy to take the drugs they are selling you, but you won't date them? Cool.

The drug game is run by Zionist Jews—yes, it is. All you have to do is run a Google search and you will see. The Zionist Jews are wealthy for a reason, and once again I will say it's not *all* Zionist Jews who have acquired their money through dodgy dealings. And might I add, not every Jew is a Zionist and not every Zionist is a Jew.

If you read up on the 'Gretchen Morgansen' report you will see how it uncovers the fact that the world's banks run on cocaine money. The global banking system runs entirely on cocaine money. So they say: "Why is the war on drugs failing?"—because they need the cash to run the banks. Why is the drug problem so rampant? Because bankers need that money to pay their bonuses.

Drug money has been said to have kept the banks afloat in its financial crisis. Vienna-based UNODC Executive Director Antonio Maria Costa said in an interview released by Austrian weekly Profil that drug money often became the only available capital when the crisis spiralled out of control last year.

"In many instances, drug money is currently the only liquid investment capital," Costa was quoted as saying by Profil. "In the second half of 2008, liquidity was the banking system's main problem and hence liquid capital became an important factor."

> *The United Nations Office on Drugs and Crime had found proof that "interbank loans were funded by money that derived from drug trade and other illegal activities," Costa was quoted as saying. There were "signs that some banks were rescued in that way."*

Ask yourself one question: whenever they show a program of them seizing a large sum of drugs on TV, have you ever seen them destroy it? Excogitate on that for a second.

The whole world is near enough corrupt; like a girl with no bum and no breast, it's a shame. I couldn't date a girl with no ass and tits, *Lard Gard*, I might as well touch myself. G-d is a proper comedian.

If your reason for not dating a man who sells drugs is because of ethics, well then you shouldn't want to date a man like me who sells alcohol because alcohol is one hell of a 'drug' and yes I will call it a drug. It sure can ruin lives just like drugs can.

When it comes to coke, understand that the same man who is sentencing Dwayne to five years is most likely the same person buying the coke. Coke is not a cheap drug, so it is most likely being sniffed by those who are upper class. Oh yes, they found traces of coke in the houses of parliament. Coke isn't cheap so you've got to have dough to afford it.

However, in saying all of that, selling drugs is illegal. The government has created a system to lock people up so they can fill up their jails and the saddest thing is that it seems to be the ethnic minorities, especially 'black' boys which they use to peddle it. Might I add, no one is forcing them. You can't get your *rampant rabbit* through customs, let alone a box of coke. We've all watched American Gangsta, so we have an idea of how the '*Christina Aguilera*' gets into the country.

As previously stated, from the guy who sells drugs to the guy who does fraud to the guy who does removals that doesn't pay tax, to Rupert Murdoch and the guys who commit white collar crimes—some people who are making money are doing so by illegal methods. I really don't like the way that drug dealers seem to get singled out a lot. It is asserted that Mr Murdoch's company got someone to hack into the phone of MillyDowler and they were deleting voicemails so new ones could come through; obviously the police then thought that the li'l girl must be alive if someone keeps deleting the voice messages. This inadvertently gave false hope to the family. *Bloodyclartswine.* It is alleged they were paying something like 600K for the information. So, as you can see, many people are doing what they are doing to make money. However, this does not make what either of them is doing right in the eyes of the law.

Mr 'Have A Fun Night With' VS Mr 'Stroll Through The Park'

I'll be straight and frank with you (talking from my point of view as a black man living in London), most of the guys you see in the club popping bottles with a table, wearing Gucci and Louis, are most likely drug dealers and fraudsters, bar the entertainers and footballers. The vast majority of them are acquiring their money illegally. A Mr Joe Bloggs who is stacking shelves in Tesco, is not likely to be popping bottles in a club and is not drowning himself in Louis and Gucci, let's be real. It's not happening. Unless he has been visiting Dagenham Dave's market stall.

There are only the select few who may have their own business or earn, like, say 3K and over after tax, and the ones who run their own business may have washed their illegal money to get that business.

Mr 'Just Getting By' most of the time isn't fun. You see a young guy in a Range, Q7 and such, more than likely it's drug money or fraud money. I am just keeping it real; I'm not weave—I really am *here*. You need to ask/probe into what he does. Most, if not all women, whether they be an artist or not, are drawn to power, and this is why women tend to be attracted to these sort of guys. Let's be real, you see a Range at the lights and you see a Clio, which car are you going to look at? "Now I know why the *chicken* crossed the road; the Clio was out of her Range".

The funniest thing is that it's either a lot of you women are naive or you just don't want to ask him what he does. If a man has no job, doesn't seem to have a trade, where else do you think he is getting his money from? Well, I tell you this for free—he isn't swinging up and down any poles.

Mr 'Just Getting By' is sweet, he really is, but 'MrDontKnowHowHe MakesHisMoneyAsLongAsICanGetMyLouisBags' is just that tad more exciting at times. But lads, you have to ask yourselves something, if you got caught, would that woman wait for you to get out? Maybe, but what if she doesn't? That means after all the treating her to the exquisite diners and the finer things in life, if you go down, someone could be *rarsing* up your missus.

I will never knock a man's hustle but one needs to know when to stop and wash that money like so many others before us have done. Some of these businesses have started on drugs, fraud money, etc. When it comes to fraud in this country no one can see the Asians but so many of them get away with it because they are smart and also because they are Asian. Damn, having 'black' skin at times can work against you—but hey, melanin to the skin is like what chlorophyll is to a plant: it converts the sun rays and turns it into energy.

The saddest thing is that the girl who goes out with Mr 'Just Getting By' guy tends to cheat on her partner with Mr 'We Can Have Fun But I Move Food By The Tonne'. If you aren't *on your thing* keep your girl out the 'West End' before they make your girl their *best friend*. Yes, there are the 'in-between guys' but I am addressing Mr illegal. No, I am not talking about Ghanaians with no stay; I mean drug dealers (and co) and Mr 'Just Getting By'.

So, you as a woman, like the drug dealers themselves, have to weigh things up. If you are dating someone who makes money illegally—and that could be someone who signs on, but does promoting on the side—yes, that is illegal too. There are many things that people do to earn money that is illegal that could land them in jail. Not that I want to digress, but I am quite sure that if I as a man was disrespecting you that you would want your man to fly in Wendy Deng style and deal with the matter and deal with it proper. Let's bear in mind if he beats me up, he could be imprisoned too.

So What Is Your Answer, Dear Rob? Spit It Out

If you are presented with the two guys I would advise for you to go with neither, but if I really want to be real, most would go for the flashy guy and just pretend to themselves that he is a businessman, even though he has no trade.

The only reason why I would say to date Mr 'Just Getting By' is if you are both on the same level. If you are more advanced than him, I would say no, the next chapter will explain why. I am giving this advice as if you were my daughter. Yes, I have broken the dynamics down, but what use is your man to you in jail? What use is the father of your kids in jail? Yes, he may never get caught, you're right, but is that a gamble you are prepared to play with your heart? I know you girls love to gamble; I can tell by the epidemic of lace front wigs—got some of you looking like a cross between a Klingon and Robocop.

I think lace front wearers should be given life, for crimes against humanity. I can't, I just can't. But jokes aside, a man who is making money illegally *can* be a good father, *can* be a great boyfriend. However, ask yourself one question: is phone sex that great? That's what it will be if he ends up inside. But we need this drug money to support the economy.

If you're looking for a man to complete you,
you've missed the whole point.

As A Woman, Does Earning Too Much Hinder My Chances Of Settling Down?

"'It makes me really uncomfortable that you make more money than me. I'm going to put that out on the table and try to get over it.'
But he never got over it, she said."

—*Whitney Hess*

I am going to get stuck straight in. No foreplay, no caressing, just straight action.

The contemporary idea of sex equality is admirable and worthy, especially in our ever-increasing civilisation, but it is not found in nature. When might is right, man hoards it over woman; when more justice, peace, and fairness prevail, she gradually emerges from slavery and obscurity. Woman's social stance has varied with the degree of militarism in any nation or age. However, man did not knowingly nor intentionally take woman's rights and then gradually and grudgingly give them back to her; all this was an unconscious and unplanned chapter of social evolution. When the point really came for women to enjoy added rights, she got them, and all quite irrespective of man's conscious attitude. Slowly, but surely, the mores change so as to adapt to the social adjustments, which are a part of the persistent evolution of civilisation.

It was science, not religion, which really disencumbered women; it was the modern factory that largely set her free from the constraints of the home. Man's physical abilities became no longer a cardinal essential in the new maintenance mechanism; science so changed the conditions of living that man power was no longer grander than woman power.

These alterations have led toward woman's liberation from domestic slavery and have brought about such a modification of her status that she now enjoys an amount of personal liberty and sex determination that practically equals a man's. Women have now been liberated; they no longer need to rely on men. Is this a good thing or a bad thing? I guess we'll let time decide.

So What Do I Believe A Man's Role To Be? What Part Is He Supposed To Play?

I will start by saying this: a woman should want a man to be a man. When she has to wear the baggy trousers and steer the ship, just know she might 'SinBad'.

I believe a man's role is to provide, protect and secure. From the primitive times, man has been a hunter. He would go out into the bush all day and night until he came home with a cat, goat, rat, whatever—no point bringing a cow home, he had one already.

Back in those times a man would have to go through a series of tests to prove to the family of the bride that he could protect her. This could mean him having to fight fellow tribe men, or having to kill an animal. Also, in these times, a man would have to stay with the bride's family for a year to prove he had the skills to be able to secure his woman. I wonder if these things should be put back in place . . .

For those who do not understand what it means to protect, provide and secure, here are the Oxford Dictionary definitions:

Protect: Keep safe from injury and harm.

For all you men that take pride in hitting women—you are clearly not protecting her. You are supposed to be keeping her safe from injury and harm, but you're finding joy in pandering her eyes.

Provide: To supply sufficient money to ensure the maintenance of someone.

Wow. Yes, wow.

To provide for your family means you must be able to give enough resources to maintain them. It's for this reason I chortle when I see men who are struggling financially trying to date successful women, and they wonder why they get rubbished. No man would want their daughter dating a broke man, but yet these same men will complain about a woman wanting someone with money. I believe it is a man's job/role to provide; it's a shame that the gender roles have been blurred somewhere down the line. Hi, Margaret Thatcher.

Secure: Feeling confident and free from fear or anxiety.

Now, if you're having bailiffs knocking on the door, have a car which always breaks down on you, then I'm sorry but it is likely your woman is not going to feel secure. Having your woman feel secure is one thing that is imperative. If she can't get that feeling from you she may get it from elsewhere. One thing I always say is: "Under-promise and Over-deliver"—women hate being let down. Being constantly let down is one thing that will make a woman not trust you.

In saying all of the above, now that the patriarchal way of living has almost been suffocated, I would say the role of a man is determined by the relationship he is in. His primary goal should be to protect his investment; that investment being his family, if he has kids with his woman. In a relationship where kids are not present, I believe his role is to simply protect his woman. Women earn now; a woman can provide for herself.

Okay, Dear Rob, What Is The Average Earnings Of Jock-Strappers And Bra-Wearers?

The average salary in the UK, according to the National Statistics survey 2010 shows that men who work fulltime, on average earn 25K a year, which means this is what the average Kunle earns, meaning the average guy who bumps into you on the street—this is what he is taking home. Yes, there may be some who will earn more and there will be some who earn less.

But if you, as a woman, earns anything more than that, it is likely you will be in trouble if you are looking to date what is deemed as a man with an average salary. If you're a woman who is earning, let's say, in excess of 60K a year—just be aware that there are a lot of men who will refuse to date you unless they are earning more than that.

Almost a third of working women out-earn men—this was bound to happen with more women going into further education than men; in saying that, there are many men who are earning money but just not registered with the Inland Revenue, if you know what I mean. However, in the corporate world, women are slowly but surely getting there.

But What The Fark, Dear Rob.
Why Should What I Earn Be A Thing?

No man wants to be rubbished (there are exceptions to the rule, but this does not disprove the rule).

Let's say you are earning 60K and he is earning 25K—you two are on different playing fields. He is Arsenal and you're Barcelona; no matter how tidy your defence is, things can get 'Messi'.

If he is earning 1.6K after tax and you are earning 3K, your money can stretch much further than his. The clothes you wear and the places you go may not fit into his budget, and most men don't want to feel inadequate when relating to their partner.

Let's just imagine you're at your Xmas dinner and it's time to pay for the bill—you slip your bank card under the table for him to pay, he gives it to the waiter and the waiter is like: "Uh, sorry, sir, this seems to be a woman's card." The way his balls will shrink.

When it's time for birthdays, even when he wants to buy you gifts, if you're a KG wearing Louis chick, as that's what your money can afford, it's going to be a struggle for you to wear a pair of shoes from Zara that he buys you for your birthday. As much as you may wear them, I doubt very much you will when doing glitz and glamour. The way those shoes will get dash to the back of the wardrobe after one wear. A man does not want to be *stunted* on while he is dating; no man wants to be embarrassed.

Let's say you're a Claridges sort of chick and he is a Pizza Express sort of guy. His money can't reach Claridges, so if you guys go on a double date with your work colleague, it will be you that has to fork the bill. Like Mark Morrison's grill—it's not a good look.

Women are credited on their beauty and how they can keep a house; men, on the other hand, are credited on wealth and power. By the woman being the bread winner, she has automatically stripped a man of that credit.

If you are earning drastically more than your man, it's you that is the umpire; he is the athlete running to the sound of your shot.

Most men like to show off; we like to impress our woman, and the way things are in society, it is done with wealth. Taking a woman to the park for a picnic because it's all you can afford is not thoughtful—it *is* thoughtful when he chooses to do that when he could have done the fancy. It is two different things. Hence, I always tell a woman that a man spending money on you means nothing if he has disposable income. When dating a man with money, it's his time and mind you need; those are the two things which he holds precious. Buying you a £300 bag is nothing, as it's just money to him.

If you live in a four-bedroom house in the country and he lives in a two-bedroom flat in an underdeveloped area, I can bet my bottom dollar you are not going to want to move in with him—and I would advise that no man moves in with a woman if he doesn't want her to turn into a bully in the playground and take his balls away. Yes, not all women are like this but from what I've researched the vast majority are.

The standard practice is that a woman moves in with the man, not vice versa. As far as I am concerned, a man should pay the bills in the house and a woman should contribute, not the other way around. I don't know what kind of man would feel comfortable contributing to the bills. He better not be doggying her and asking: "Who's the man, who's the man?"—I am sorry, dude, you *aren't* the man. She is providing, protecting and securing you, therefore *she* is the man of the house.

We can all sit here and pretend that money doesn't matter, but money is power—period. A broke man cannot throw his weight around. That's why I chortle when I see women allow broke men to give them the run around—and no, I am not taking shots at men who are not doing well for themselves. But with the definition of what a man is meant to be—like an asthmatic with no pump, you're struggling slightly.

Family Issues

You could meet the girl of your dreams, but you will find that if you are marrying into a wealthy family they may turn their nose up against you. Love is great; however, I am not letting any man who can't Protect, Provide and Secure my daughter marry her. Hell to the MF no. So, what happens when you impregnate her and she is on maternity leave? Please, I beg go that way>>>>>>>>>>>>>Now jump off the cliff<<<<<<<<<. Okay, it's time for you to get married, and as the woman, you have to contribute to the wedding ring you want—*and* to the dress you want; if you're a 100K a year chick—yeah, love is great, but I doubt very much you are going to want to wear a 1K wedding ring. You most probably have jewellery that costs that. Once again, a man may feel inadequate; the lifestyle that the family have given to her, if you as a man cannot match that, you may be in trouble. Most dads are not interested in all that love *ish* for their daughter. They are interested in whether you can provide, protect and secure her. If they realise that you aren't bringing anything to the table, apart from your short arms and deep pockets, you may be dismissed nicely.

If as a man you were raised in a home where dad was the breadwinner, it's going to be very difficult for such man to now allow a woman to steer the ship. He isn't used to it; he doesn't know what it means for a woman to be calling the shots, hence he may not want to date a woman who is making more money than him. As much as we can say that a woman doesn't need to be in control when earning more than the man, I'll be damned if I am a woman bringing in the majority of the income and a man is telling me what to spend the money on; sorry, it isn't happening.

What Have You Done For Me Lately?

It's sad to say that all these man-bashing songs that the likes of Pastor Beyoncé Knowles have sung in the past have caused a huge problem. The whole 'Can you pay my bills?' nonsense, and: 'If not, you and me can't chill' has led/made so many women pretentious. To the point that so many men would never even dream of dating a woman who is a high earner. What happens when this song comes on when we are in the house? All this independent woman nonsensical nonsense is yet another thing that has put a man's back against the wall.

All these battery power packed anthems have given women this unnecessary form of ego, which is not needed. You are not an independent woman if you know how to pay your bills; it means you are an adult. How many times do you hear a man saying he is an independent man? It's okay, I can wait. It's these sorts of songs and renditions that have put so many men in the mind-set of not wanting his woman to earn drastically more than him. The last thing a man wants is to be rubbished. You driving, living by yourself and paying your bills means you're an adult; it's what adults do.

I have been in shit cars and the rubbishing I have got from girls who were in nicer cars isn't a joke. They look at me, smile and then take a look back at the car and I can just see their brain thinking: "Computer Says No". Any man who has driven nice cars and driven bangers will tell you the difference having money makes. Two identical twins at the traffic lights: one is in a Range, the other in a Clio—who are you going to give the time of day to? The question doesn't even need answering.

I am no saint, but one thing no girl can ever call me is a wasteman. I have never ponced off a woman; never tried to live in her house. Nope, sorry, not this dude. You can call me a *gallis*, a player, a womaniser, whatever, but you can never call me a wasteman. If you're about to date a woman whose boyfriend was on his thing, a highflyer—and you aren't saying much . . . may the force be with you. It has been proven that men find it hard to go back sexually, and women find it hard to go back lifestyle-wise. If her man had his own place, took holidays three times a year, bought her nice gifts, took her nice places, it will be hard for her to go back to farking in your mum's house and going to Nando's. Money may not be able to buy you love, but it will buy you things that girls will love you for. A woman can get comfortable with money.

Women who earn a lot tend to work long days, some up to thirteen hours. You can't expect a woman who has done this to come home and do the cleaning, cooking, etc. She will *not* and this is where problems may occur. Gender roles have shifted; the housekeeping is no longer being solely done by women, as some are too busy. Yes, some can juggle, but if we have both had a hard long day at work, a man cannot expect a woman to be doing the cooking. I wouldn't expect my woman to come home and cook after doing a thirteen hour shift. It's not fair. I need her for the bedroom. She can put her brain to good use in there.

No man ever wants to be told off by his woman for not pulling his weight, unless she is a personal trainer; hence, dating a woman who has more drive than you can be a problem. I have heard several women say the reason they left their partner was because they outgrew him. This simply means she is somewhere in life where he isn't.

Plain and simple.

Okay, So You've Rambled On, But Where To From Here, Dear Rob?

In the ideals of pair marriage, woman has eventually won acknowledgement, distinction, equality, and education; but will she prove worthy of all this new and aberrant accomplishment? Will the contemporary woman respond to this phenomenal achievement of social liberation with idleness, indifference, barrenness, and infidelity? Today, in the twenty-first century, woman is undergoing the crucial test of her long world journey!

Each sex has its own peculiar sphere of existence, together with its own rights within that sphere. If women keep hankering to enjoy all of man's rights, then, sooner or later, emotionless competition will displace chivalry and special consideration, which many women now enjoy, and which they have so recently won from men.

Civilisation can never annihilate the behaviour hiatus between the sexes. From age to age, the mores change, but instinct doesn't. Innate maternal affection will never allow emancipated woman to become man's serious rival in industry. Forever each sex will remain cardinal in its own domain, domains determined by biological differentiation and by mental disparity.

Many women who are high flyers in their industry seem to not have kids. Being a woman, as stated, already hinders one's progress in the working environment as the maternal instinct is innate in most women. I know so many young female teachers who, because of their workload, have said they are not sure about having kids.

There was a season of The Apprentice where a woman who had a cleaning company would go out to bring home the bacon while the man took care of the home and looked after the kids. Now, this works for them, but I don't see this working for many a man because of the physical nature of a man and the maternal nature of a woman; woman has been led to the home and man to the field to work.

If the hours you work impinge on the upkeep of the home, it will cause a problem even if you and your partner earn the same. If times get hard and you as the woman are the breadwinner, it only makes sense for him to quit work and stay at home looking after the child. It has to be something your man is prepared to do. I am not sure many a man will be happy doing that, but with the way things are going and the fact that a third of women are now bringing in more than men, coupled with the fact that in the UK and most parts of the western world women outnumber men—as Giggs would say: "Jheeeeze", can you 'Imogen' the problems women who are earning a lot are going to face?

The truth is that with the way women have been liberated, so many of them have got on their low donkeys, which has pushed so many men against the wall. As stated, all this independent nonsense has made man further say to himself: "If I can't do more for her than she can do for herself then it's long". No man wants to be rubbished by a woman, and secretly, when you have to pull a man along, you slyly lose respect for him; not in all cases, but many.

A man who meets a woman who is a high flyer and who works crazy hours is just going to have to be prepared to be a house husband, or pay for a nanny to look after the kids. As for me, I am not having any nanny looking after my kids—nope, sorry. Women have been liberated, yes, but I get a joy in being able to provide for my woman and family. I can't have a woman taking that upon herself. I just can't.

This is where men need to buck up their ideas and hasten to the way the world is changing. If we as men allow women to start earning more than us, and becoming the man of the house, then we are going to have to take our roles in the kitchen; cooking and cleaning, as well as doing the school run, while our women go out to work.

No one can tell a human being to *not* aspire to succeed, so I would never say to women to stop achieving; it's men that need to pull up their pants, because if this shift occurs, many a man are going to find themselves in the kitchen—or more and more women will be single.

A man's ego will certainly not allow most men to live off a woman, or be beneath her; it's just what makes us men. There are some who can do this; there are many men who can, but I don't see an alpha male dating a woman who earns significantly more than him. If you as a woman are earning more than him—you are the provider. You are the man of the house, as you are earning the bulk of the money. It's more than likely that you will be the decision maker.

Both of us can't be working crazy hours—not saying that all well-paid jobs that women do require long hours, but most of them do—and if these long hours restrict you from your womanly duties at home, you are going to encounter problems.

This new shift is going to be interesting. One needs to see whether man can adapt to this or whether more and more women are just going to find themselves single. You never know, toy boys may become the new craze as seen by so many of these cougars.

If you're looking for a man to complete you,
you've missed the whole point.

Mummy, Who's That Maaaaaaaaaaaaaaaaaaaaaan?

**"It is easier to build strong children
than to repair broken men."**

—Frederick Douglass

In my short life, I have dated women with kids, and the things I have seen some do is shocking; more shocking than women who wear tights and try and pass them off as leggings. Yes, I have *clocked*, it's YUCKIE.

One thing I think a lot of women seem to forget is that kids are not stupid; they are not.

The Don'ts When Dating A Man When You Have Kids

Your children should not be in the house when you're letting a man stroke your cat; this is foul play and is a bookable offence. Many times in the past I have been at a woman's house and the child has almost burst in. It is foul play. Yes, your kitty may be purring for some wood, but taking hood while your kids are around is no good. Any man with any decency will not rate you.

Secondly, it is highly frustrating when a man is just about to slip it in and then you have to leave to attend to your baby crying. This is one thing some of us men talk about behind your backs—just giving you the heads up.

It's for this reason I say women with kids should date men who have their own place. Random men really shouldn't be all up in your house, especially when you have children.

He's Just A Link, Why Is He Meeting Your Kids?

As previously stated, kids aren't stupid; they really are not. Kids from the age of two can get attached and become familiar. If said dude is not your man, does he need to meet your kids? If he is just knocking boots, do your kids need to know his shoe size? I am very good with kids and they seem to get attached to me. I have had too many incidences in the past where girls I have exchanged bodily fluids with, have had their kids asking after me, to the point where they've called me to speak to them. As much as I am cool with that, not every man is like me. I can see the excitement in the li'l boys' eyes when I play football with them or play fight with them. I can see them yearning for that father figure. The last thing you want as a woman is your child getting attached to a link.

I guess me being so 'open' has got her child getting so 'close'. It's going to hurt him when he doesn't see me around.

Nah, It's Cool, I'll Drop Her At Sandra's

Help us to respect you. Dropping your child at Sandra's, Lakeisha's, Andrea's, so that you can *tek* body will not get you respected by a man. If you can drop your child at x y z at the drop of the hat to get sex, it will not put you in a good light. In having a child comes responsibility and sacrifices.

In my filthy years while raving in Birmingham, I've had some crazy experiences. I once met this girl on a Friday night; by Saturday afternoon she was at my hotel. I went down to the reception, and lo and behold, I saw a baby carrier next to her. I was like: "What the hell? What's that?" I was vex, because I was thinking: *'Man definitely ain't getting his head wet today.'* I was grumpy, I was angry, I was downtrodden, I felt betrayed. So anyway, she makes her way upstairs to my hotel room like a lamb to the slaughter. She puts the baby carrier by the door, jumps on the bed and we begin watching TV. Thirty minutes of chilling goes by, and then she asks me if I want a massage. I thought to myself: *Massage? Does this girl actually want to fark? Does she want 'de ting'? 'Je Nike'?* So I dropped the top like a Ferrari on a hot summer's day. *Man's got segseeborrie u gets me. You know, fine boy one pimple.* Anyway, my girl starts massaging me and it was like 'Go-go-gadget dick'—my boy rose to attention, sprung out like Jack in the box.

She had awoken the beast. *Egorh' is h' alive.* Now, I, for one second did not think this girl was going to have sex with me, especially not with her five-month-old daughter here. My eyes were shut, and then I felt a wet warm sensation on my hood. I looked up and my girl was backing me head. At the time this happened I was a durty dog (2009), so I actually couldn't give two farts. Cut a long story short, we ended up having sex with her child in the room facing the wall. Now this girl will expect a man to take her serious. Well, not after you brought your daughter to a hotel room to meet a guy you met the night before. You can't chase dick when you have kids; like a girl with no bum and no *breastisis,* it doesn't look good.

I have had girls in the past tell me they will come to my house with their child—"the child can play in the front room; all I have to do is give him/her some toys and he's cool."

I'm A Glamour Model, And What?

Once again, my plea is: *help us to respect you*. How can you teach your son to respect a woman when you, as his mum, have your tits and ass out of doors like an Avon catalogue? I implore you to read up on Sara Baartman. Her story will explain to you why women get exploited the way they do in Hip-Hop. Her story is deep. There is a reason why it only seems like it's 'black' music like Bashment, Hip-Hip, so on and so forth, where they find pleasure in degrading their women. Read up on her; it will enlighten you. I don't know what man in his right mind would want to date a woman who has kids and decides to parade her body for men to ogle over. However, in saying that, there are some men who condone this bollocks. It's quite sad, as us men shouldn't advocate this, especially when a woman has a child. My heart almost cried when I watched UK Hip-Hop hunnies—and that girl was parading herself in front of her son; it was embarrassing. If you want to strip and you have no kids by all means do your thing, but if you *do* have kids . . .?

It just makes no sense to me.

My Baby Father Is A *Beep Beep*

Constantly slating the father of your child on Twitter, Facebook, or to a potential partner is not a good look. Just remember it was you that slept with this person that you're calling a *wasteman*. No one coerced you, no one forced you. No matter what sales pitch you give a guy, the father of your child is a perfect example of what kind of guy you go for, or have gone for. It speaks volumes. If you can be slating the father of your child all over social mediums, then surely if you and I fall out, you can do the same. I'm okay, thanks. I'll pass on this occasion. As much as the father of your child may be a cock head/wankstain, slating him to a link or a potential partner is not a good look. Also, it makes you sound a tad bitter. The best form of revenge is to show him you're in a better place than he left you. You can't say you're truly over someone until you have moved on from the place in which you were left. Bickering over him just shows he still has a hold on you. And as a man, I don't want to know that the father of your child can affect our relationship. I don't want to know that one minute you can be in a good mood and then the next in a foul one because of what he has said.

So, Dear Rob, When Would You Say Is The Right Time To Introduce A Man To My Children?

Never! No, I'm only joking. If this man is just going to be a *fark buddy*, a link, then he does not need to meet your children. I don't care if you're running late to pick them from school. Your kids don't need to see him. Kids are not stupid, hence the title: "Mummy, who's that maaaaaaaaaaaaaaaan?" As stated earlier, the last thing you want is your kids getting attached to a link—and secondly, kids talk. If their father is still in their life, the last thing you want is for them telling the father of their child about all these different men in your life. It's not a good look; not at all. If you are going to have sex, I implore you to go on the pill and, even then, use a condom. You don't want to fall pregnant for a guy who doesn't want to start a family with you. Having two kids with two different fathers may inadvertently blacklist you. If, and when, a man is ready to commit to you, is when I believe he should be introduced to your kids; other than that, I don't feel there is any need. You don't want your kids seeing different men in and out of your house. And if your Kitty Kat is itching so much and you just need to *tekbody*, can you make sure he doesn't stay over? As much as you don't want to feel cheap, the last thing you want your kids doing is bumping into him while he is leaving the bathroom in his boxers. It's awkward for us guys and also for your child—if they are of age.

In saying all of the above, when you have a child who is under the age of one, if we want to be honest, it's highly unlikely that they are going to know what is going on, but it's more for the man. I wouldn't want to know that the mother of my child is having sex while my child is in the house. If you're capable of doing it now, then I guess if I give you a child and we aren't together you may do the same.

You've got to help *us* to help *you*; the way you conduct yourself around your child is a clear indication of how you will behave if I had a child with you. If this is how you are going to behave if we break up—I'm okay, thanks. She can get out of my **boat**, I don't want to **Noah**.

A man has no right to label a woman who has two baby fathers as loose, especially when he and his brother have different dads—what does that make his mum?

Let me slip this in quickly before closing: why would you have a full blown conversation with a man when you've just picked up your child from school? What is the meaning of this? Yes, it may be **raining,** but that's not an excuse to have **hood** on your head. Some of us men pay attention to this. This should be common sense, but common sense isn't common.

If you're looking for a man to complete you,
you've missed the whole point.

You're Not My Daddy

**"I cannot think of any need in childhood as strong as the
need for a father's protection."**

—Sigmund Freud

Hmm, well, well, well. Men generally don't want anyone penetrating the mother of their child. The amount of times I've had close calls is no joke. I've had to pretend to be cousins; I've pretended to be a mechanic. Dating a woman with kids is not easy, especially when the father of the child is still in the picture. If the man is still interested in you, I am not interested, sorry. I am not involved. I would go as far as saying if he is not in jail, doing life, or dead, I am not involved. It is hard enough dating a woman, than to have external factors working against my relationship. I met a nice lady in 2010; she had a lovely daughter and was a good woman herself. One day I was chilling at home, being cool as usual, then my cellular rings. I look at the phone. I didn't recognise the number, but answered anyhow. It's her ex/father of her child. The guy came on the phone, talking a whole heap of Kilimanjaro gangster talk, telling me he wants to kidnap me, tie me up, blah, blah, blah, telling me that I am the one that is stopping him and the mother of his child getting together; that *I* am breaking up a happy family. Dude was asking me for my address; he wanted my postcode. He lived in the midlands. He then proceeded to tell me who he knew in London and who he would get to wrap me up. Funniest thing is, the names he was reeling off—I knew who they were. After going back and forward with this guy, he then broke down on the phone. I was in stitches. Dude started pleading with me that he wants to start a family with her. He said if I could just fall back like Jamie Fox's hairline, he would be ever so gracious. The dude went from wanting to put me to sleep like a baby and kidnap me, to asking me questions of where he may be going wrong. I felt for the dude. He wanted to be with mother of his child but she no longer wanted to be with him, and as far as he was concerned I was the one hindering his progress. Sad times. I could reel off a million-and-one stories that mates of mine have been involved in, when the father of the woman's child has caught them in the house. I've had friends who have had to jump out windows. Most men do not want a next man sleeping with the mother of their child, especially when they are still in love with them, or wants to be with them. This is one of the reasons why I said, like a broken frame, the dude needs to be out of the picture. I don't want to hear his voice or see him. I'm okay, thanks. I don't want to get wrapped up like Christmas Eve. Of course, not all men who have kids for a woman are like this.

I'm Going To Tell My Daddy About You

I took a poll and asked whether a man is allowed to slap/smack/physically reprimand another man's child and ninety-percent of the respondents said no, that a man should not reprimand another man's child. So I should put another man's child in my house, fend for the child financially, emotionally, but when he is out of line or misbehaving I am not allowed to reprimand the child physically? Let's say the child is mocking my existence and needs reprimanding? I shouldn't? Cool, you're having a laugh. I am not involved. If that is the case, I don't want to date a woman with kids. If you're telling me this child can be taking me for Ben Sherman and I'm meant to just take it, then nah, I'm okay thanks. I will put the child in a sharp shooter.

This is not going down, not on my clock. From when the kid knows I can't do anything to him, then he is going to mock me. You better date another man, I am not raising a child when I can't reprimand him/her. And truth be told, most men would not want a next man smacking their child; they wouldn't. This is yet another reason why a lot of men tend to shy away from women with kids.

Let me just picture the scene: I smack her son for being naughty and then five minutes he walks in with the phone in his hand and says: "My dad wants to speak to you." *Farda Lord Jezuz*, hell will break loose. And that is the reality of it; a child can tell me: "Don't smack me, you're aren't my daddy."

Feel Free To Raise My Child, Just Remember They Have My Surname

That's what the biological father said to the stepdad; and he told me, upon hearing that, he had to bail. And it was when he relayed this conversation that it dawned on me—because, in essence, what he is saying is true: you can have a child living in your house, under your roof, pump X-amount of money into him, put him on the right path, take him to soccer school, and make a baller out of him . . . But when that child makes it, it's the father's surname that will be on display. When the guy in the barber shop broke this down to me, my heart sunk. How can I take a child under my wing, only for him to be promoting his father's legacy? It's the family surname that lives on. If I am going to be with a woman with kids, the child will have to change their surname to mine. I don't care. I am going to fend for this child like it is mine, so why can't the child have my family name? When you adopt a child, the child usually takes your surname. If said child is living with me, the child will see me more than their biological father. The child wakes up to me every morning. If the child has the father's surname I have no legal right to that child. I need some rights *dag nam it*.

In speaking to so many men, this has become the harsh reality that you could raise another man's child and he will get all the credit for it. I can't. I'm sorry.

We're Going To Disneyland, Florida. Oh, And You're Not Invited

Call me insecure, but I am sorry, I am not having it. If I date a woman with kids, she is not going on holiday with the father of her child. If their little child says that for his birthday he/she wants to go Disneyland and wants his dad to come along, it's not happening, not on my Breitling; you're having a bubble and shake, and who am I not to allow the child their request? Situations like this have occurred where a friend of mine was seeing a girl—the father of the child had booked tickets for Alton Towers for the child (it was his birthday) and the mother. The package which he had booked involved them spending the night at Alton Towers; even though they had separate rooms, my mate wasn't too chuffed. In this scenario, the dad was very active in the child's life and wanted to do things as a family and every so often would arrange family outings which would obviously ostracise him. What a life. This is another reason why the men I have spoken to have said that the dad would have to be out of the picture completely. What a life we lead. What a life we live.

Ask yourself one question: would you let your partner go to Disneyland, Florida, with the mother/father of their child for the child's birthday?

All Isn't Lost

There *are* men out there who will be with a woman with kids; I am just shedding light on the others who refuse to. In speaking with them, what I have mentioned above has been the reality of it. I take my hat off; if I was a woman, I'd take my lace wig off to any man who can take on the responsibility of raising a next man's child. I rate him to the fullest. It's no easy feat.

If you're a woman with kids, all is not lost: there are men out there who don't mind dating a woman with kids. But we have to be honest, when you had no kids yourself you were probably opposed to dating someone with kids. So one should be able to understand the reason why some don't favour the situation.

If you're looking for a man to complete you,
you've missed the whole point.

Bareback Riders Vs. I Hate My Baby Father

"You educate a man; you educate a man. You educate a woman; you educate a generation."

—Brigham Young

Hey, barebackers, I see you. Yeah, I see you.

Yes, as the title suggests, I am talking about men and women who like to play the victim role. As adults we are all aware of what happens when a man and woman have sex unprotected. Is this a new phenomenon? Are you only discovering that bareback riding could lead to you being attached to this woman/man for the rest of your life? Three minutes of passion for a lifetime commitment. Is it really worth it? You knew he ran up in you raw and you never thought to take the Morning After Pill? I'll tell you why: because you wanted the baby. Yes, you did. A woman knows whose child she will keep and not keep. Is it not your womb? Have you not placed a value on it? And you men who love to put your future in a woman's hand—you're funny. How can you complain when you decided to let your **semen,** no **David,** swim up her stream? How?

Like, she never told you she was on the pill and then you just decided to splash water palace style . . .? *'Wetting be up wid you?'* . . . *'Ah, what kind of nonsensical nonsense?'*

102

When you run up on a woman bareback, what you are saying is: "Here is my future, do as you wish with it." A woman can do whatever she wants with HER—yes, *her*—body. All you've done is transferred your seed *inside her* soil. As much as it is your seed, it is her soil and that is one thing us men need to come to the realisation of. Ask **Eddie Murphy,** I'm not being **delirious**.

But I Hear The Men Screaming At Me Now: "But What If She Says She Is On Contraception?"

To which I say: "Brother, let's not forget it was Eve who gave Adam the apple." We live in a day and age where one can't trust anybody. If she is not your girl, you should not be barebacking her; like that time of the month—PERIOD—you should not, and it's the same for you bra-wearers. No matter how sweet the shish kebab might taste, you can't be letting any Kunle, Dapo or Craig worship in your coven unprotected. Are you not scared of HIV? As a link, you owe each other no commitment; if he wants to stroke another Sheba, he can.

I have been *shotted* once before by some broad who looked like cum couldn't melt in her mouth—and since that day, I said *fark this shit*. The bloody trick made me shot my whole camp. I had girls ringing me like "We need to talk," and, women, we all know what that means, don't we? Oh, and no, I never got *shotted* the clap, thank G-d. It was trichomonas, a simple infection—"we tank G-d". Lads, you have to be careful; these girls have turned into *trapstars*—they are *shotting* man left right and centre.

Fark My Baby Father—Pun Not Intended. "Well, You Already Have, Darling"

Please, please, *please* stop with this baby father slating. Did anyone beg you to sleep with him? Were you coerced? Were you cajoled? If you weren't in a relationship with him, like Superman, you have no legs to stand on. It was a *fark* and that was it. Yes, a *fark*, a bit of dick, take it for what it was. If a man decides to stay, it is up to him. I am tired of hearing this: "Oh, he is a wasteman" talk. Was he not a wasteman when he was stroking your cat? What, did you expect him to change? Half of the time, when a man is sleeping with a link, he couldn't care less about her. Stop trying to play the victim role. If you were not in a relationship with this dude, he owes you and the child in your belly nada. Yes, nada. In this England we live in, a man has near enough no rights to that child. None. If a man decides to stay you should run in the street naked and scream for joy. And if we want to talk on the line of metaphysics, the child belongs to neither of you, it belongs to the universe. Nature knows nothing of what is fair; all it is concerned about is reproduction.

It is your womb, your body, and it is *you* that is left with the responsibility. Have some of you not grasped this yet? A man does not have to stay. How do you expect him to form a bond with a child when he doesn't even know you? The only reason you can form a bond with that child is because you carried him/her for nine months—let's be real. You think some random could just dump a child on you and you would be able to feel a connection . . .? Let's not be saxicolous on this matter.

Not all BMs are the same, hence why we have '3 series, 5 series,' etc. If you were just a link, then zip it. Thank you very much, cheers.

It's only those who were in relationships that should be hooting and tooting. You girls that were links . . . prop your pillow and lay in your bed. Thank you very much, amen. G-d is good and so is Chambord.

Oh, lads, if you want to introduce a drink to a girl and impress her, Chambord is the one. Thank me later, but make sure you bloody strap up like Rambo; in fact, like Arnie; in fact, like James Bond—that mofo *never* seems to get touched.

But Why Do So Many Of These Guys Bareback?

Truth be told, many man bareback because they have problems getting up—and no, I'm not talking about alarm clock getting up. No, I mean they have erectile dysfunction. As in, they can't get it hard.

So, some men just think *fark it*: I'm not missing out on this beat; I refuse to be an acapella, *fark that*—now I am hard, *man's* slipping that straight down the cat's throat. Then three weeks later he gets the late text for not using his **latex**. Now he wants to **'rubber'** of her child; oh, the irony. Oh, what a sad state of affairs.

Men, we have to take some ownership of this—it's a 50/50 thing. You give a woman your semen she can do what the hell she wants with it; whatever she wishes. She can swallow it, spit it out—or decide to have a baby. The moment you let your **bad boys** swim in her stream it's likely you're going to be a **puff daddy**—so get that **dirty money** ready.

It's funny how so many women are pro-choice, but yet whine and moan when men run off. Well, you decided to not want to face responsibility and so did he. Another funny thing is that when a woman aborts a child that a man wants, no one really bats an eyelid, as it's *her* body. Hmm, her body . . . *Your* body, *your* child. Cool.

Where To From Here?

We are adults. We know what happens when we have unprotected sex. It was for this reason, in the primitive ages, that no sex before marriage was implemented; because of humans acting like the animals they are. It's lions that roam around the jungle, just beating anything, but then again, I guess a **tiger wood** if he's on **par**; I'm not **lion** ask **Mufasa.**

Men, I would boldly say we have to stop leaving our future in the hands of women. Once you release your semen *inside her* body, she can do what the hell she wants and you can't stop her. And when she decides to have that kid, she also can do whatever she wants.

Oh, and before I close, if you have had an abortion or made a woman have one you have no right talking down to single mothers. The only reason you aren't one is because you played Arnold swat-a-fella and terminated the foetus.

The Sex Lottery Of STIs

Along with pregnancy is also the fear of catching an STI—or, even worse, HIV. Kids, I can't afford HIV. I can't. As sweet as skin-to-skin contact may feel, catching a case isn't. I often ask myself: are we really that scared of contracting HIV? Well, we can't be *that* scared as the vast majority of us sleep with people without checking their current status. If we really want to be honest with ourselves, we shouldn't be bareback riding until one has checked one's sexual health. Wow, we really are trusting humans, aren't we? The one time I ever contracted something was from one girl who looked like an angel—bloodyclart Delilah. Well, she tricked me; she gave me a nice dose of trichomonas. *Kilo Mike Tango*. As they say, looks can be deceiving and she sure deceived me. The swine flu of a woman gave me an infection—but, hey, I can't blame her. It takes two to tango. Why was I sleeping with her raw? Why didn't I use my rain coat? And guess what I did like a prick? I ended up giving it to someone else. I felt like shit. I felt like craps. Up until today I feel like such a mug. The embarrassment of giving someone an STI is not funny. Ladies, you shouldn't be sleeping unprotected with someone who isn't your man. You shouldn't. The sex lottery is no joke. In the UK, according to the United Kingdom statistics, around 86,500 people were living with HIV in the UK at the end of 2009, of which a quarter of them were unaware of their infection. Highlighting word: UNAWARE. Now, that sends a shiver down my spine. But at the same time it is obvious; some people may not be aware that they have contracted the virus. Let me just throw this in there for good measure: it is alleged that the HIV virus is a man-made disease, and that it was invented in a lab by a man called Dr Robert Gallo. Some refer to AIDS as AmericasInfectiousDisease. But that's another discussion for another topic. Oh, might I just throw this in while we're on the subject of HIV? Africans never contracted HIV by sleeping with monkeys—no, they never. I would go as far as to say they were infected *with* HIV. There were no AIDS in Africa pre-colonisation. So how did this virus all of a sudden find its way to the continent? Sounds a bit like biological warfare. Google Dr Robert Gallo in your own time and see what you make of things. And while we're on the topic of biological warfare—in your own time, do a Google search on eugenics/maafa 21. It will uncover some shocking truths about abortion. Was this another form of genocide? Was this another avenue used to kill off people of colour? Was it man-made, so it could be used as another form of population control? Feel free to Google a woman called Margeret Sanger, too. It will open your eyes and uncover one of the main reasons why abortion was legalised. Abortion is not and should not be used as a form of contraception.

Any who, ladies, you have to be aware that a lot of men are sleeping with more than one woman at the same time. A lot of men are, so it's in your best interest to tell a brother to strap up like car seats. Only G-d knows where all these STIs came from . . .

Babes, I'm Tired, Can We Have Sex Tomorrow?

Watch out for these tactics. It is very unlikely that a man will be too tired to have sex; very rare. Why is he tired? Maybe it's because he's contracted something? And I don't mean business-wise. I know a lot of men who have caught something, and to avoid sleeping with their missus, have brought their little kid into the bed. There are some men who will go to the clinic, get the tablets for you, and put it in your drink in the morning. Oh, the games that us men play at times. But yeah, if your man who loves head, all of a sudden is opposed to it, it might suggest he's holding and doesn't want to give you a dose. Seeing as we're on the topic of head, it's funny how a lot of you women will let a man sleep with you, but you won't give him head. Are you saying that your mouth is more valuable than your womb/vagina? Okay. So you'd happily let a man put his thermometer inside your princess purse but you won't give him head just yet? Bit backwards, don't you think?

In saying that, might I add, one's mouth is more delicate a region than the vagina and can actually be more vulnerable to bacteria and viruses. STIs like chlamydia, genital herpes, gonorrhoea, hepatitis B and genital warts can all be contracted from oral sex. So if you're one of those girls who make a man use a condom because you're scared of disease, but still give fellatio—you still could catch a **case**, so it might make sense for him to put a **Johnnie** on his **Coch**ran before you **solicit** any activity with your mouth, if you don't know his sexual state.

Happy days.

If you're looking for a man to complete you,
you've missed the whole point.

We Love A Girl With A Good Head On Her Shoulders

(That Knows How To Succeed)

"Good sex is like good bridge. If you don't have a good partner, you'd better have a good hand."

—*Mae West*

Sometimes my wordplay goes over heads like condoms, like the title of this chapter. Read it back and you might get it.

Most, if not all men, will find it hard to go back sexually; meaning, if their ex was a freak in the sheets, and you're a prude, you may find the man you're dating may lose interest in you. Just remember if *you* won't, *she* will, ask Drake. A lot of people like to play down the importance of sex. Well, the pornography industry is a billion-dollar industry according to Adult Industry Trade Association; the line "Sex Sells" is no joke. "She wasn't very book smart, dead brain cells, but she still ended up making money—well, I guess brain cells."

Sex involves pleasing one another at the same time; this exchange of pleasure creates gratitude and affection which inadvertently deepens human relations and creates a union between two people emotionally. Sexual pleasure between two consenting adults does not require any justification; when one isn't getting good sex, it is highly likely that one will get if from somewhere else. When most women are single, or in a relationship where their man can't fulfil them, they tend to use their vibrator to assist them. One of the reasons why I tell men not to complain if their woman uses a vibrator—it could be that instrument that is saving your relationship or stopping her from cheating. Men, on the other hand, tend to stray when their lioness can't/or can no longer fulfil their needs.

Sex can be likened to hunger in the sense that one can have an appetite for it. When it needs to be quenched, it needs to be quenched, but it differs slightly as it is interpersonal. Though at times someone may be used as a sexual object and therefore a man may get tired of sleeping with the same woman, this is not necessarily the same for his sex drive. It's for this reason that a woman needs to try to do her best to keep her man stimulated and interested. As the saying goes: "There's no pussy better than new pussy". Sex is what happens when two humans are aroused by one another. It is an innate propensity.

Sex is an art; it is something which needs to be learned. One can't assume that they are good at whatever they do. I've come across women in the past (excuse the pun) whose sex was stale like gone off bread. I mean, how can you just lay there on your back like you're on a sunbed machine? What is the meaning of this? So, while I'm putting work in like 9-5, bussing out my back, you think you can just lay there? No babes, not round here. You better squeeze my bum cheeks, wiggle about, do *something*. Yes, most men may want a bad *bish* in the bedroom, but that doesn't mean you can play dead like a dog. You've got it all wrong. Sex is a two way thing; it is important that you participate, get involved, it's a team effort. One thing that I have discovered that annoys some men is women who just lay there, like the opposite of "that time of the month"—it's not on. You need to get involved.

There are many positions when it comes to sex; missionary is not the only one. Feel free to jump on top, ride him and drive him crazy. One has to be sexually confident. Show your sexual prowess. If you haven't got a clue what to do, simply flick on a porno, watch how some women do their stuff. Or invest in a book about sexual positions. Sex can make and break a relationship before it even starts. If the sex is wack, the propensity of him staying around in your circle is square.

Oral Sex

Yes, we may dislike **flowers** but our hoods love **tulips**. Oh, we do love the wetness. In my short time on Urantia I have heard some 'wombmans' say that they don't give head. Huh? What? Pardon? I thought they stopped making women like you in 2000. You don't want to give head? Cool. It's not by force; if *you* won't, *she* will. It's as simple as that. It's not by force. But what am I meant to tell my penis? "Sorry, pal, you won't be getting any mouth hugs from her, sorry." Oh, the heartache; oh, the pain. I understand that some of you women may see it as disgusting—well, boy, unfortunately you are an anomaly. All men love good head—so I would say it is in your best interest to satisfy his needs. The best way to start . . . is to just start. One just has to overcome whatever fears they may have.

Now, you can't perform on a dry apparatus. You must keep it nice and wet; this is the only time when you are allowed to spit on a man. Keep the apparatus nice and moist. Nothing worse than a woman giving you head on a dry dick. Are you trying to start a fire or something with all that friction?

A lot of you lovely ladies seem to get your teeth in the way. Yes, we may be eager like a beaver to get some head but it doesn't mean that we want it to feel like you have the teeth of one—I'll be damned. If you need to practice on an ice lolly, feel free to see if you leave any teeth marks on it. A lot of men may not tell you that it's actually hurting. You may just find that when you want to give him head, he's not very keen paddy, no Roy. "Nah, babes, you don't have to do that, let's just have sex." A man who likes head shouldn't be opposed to receiving head, he shouldn't—so that should be an indication that some thing's up (apart from the obvious). As you women are fully aware, a lot of you fake 'coming', but us men rarely do. If you don't see him freeze up like a hold up or see his feet clench like a fist when giving his 'life' man-hugs then you may be doing something wrong. Oh, and ladies, we love the eye contact. It's sexy. I am still yet to find a man that can keep eye contact with a woman while she is giving him head. That's some sexy ish right there. It's good to get **ahead** of yourself. You don't need to be scientist to experiment with a few condiments. Feel free to use some syrup or any flavoured sauce you like if that might help you. We like a woman who gives **head freely;** we don't want to have to take it by force like a **guillotine**.

Doorags, Headscarves And Long T-shirts

What is the meaning? Is this the method of seduction that you have chosen to ravish him with? I beg go and face the wall. I understand that you may want to keep your hair looking purty but I don't want to picture Ja Rule or Mark Morrison when you jump in the bed. This is not going down. You have to keep it hot. You can't be jumping in the bed with that stuff on your head if you want sex—nope, sorry. The **mack** will not be **returning**. He may turn his back on you and drop sleep. I have heard many women complaining that their man doesn't seem interested in sex, etc. Well, with the way you've jumped into bed, you don't seem interested yourself. Once the sex is over, feel free to fling your doorag, burkha or headscarf on—not beforehand. Oh, and for you ladies that refuse to have sex because you don't want to sweat your hair out, get a life before he gets one with someone else.

Suspenders, stocking, heels—oh, we love that ish, we sure do . . . for all of the five seconds that it may be on you before it hits the floor, we love it. Sadly, the porno industry seems to have distorted the realities of sex, so some of us men have seen the images portrayed in these scenes and want them enacted. Some of us need to be stimulated; after having sex with the same woman for a matter of years it is possible for a man to lose interest slightly in his mate. Yes it is. We can sit here and try and pretend that love covers all. Yeah, yeah, yeah. It has been said that in humans the neurochemical bases of early stage romantic love may be substantially different from those of longer term romantic relationships, with most intense stages lasting somewhere between eighteen to thirty-six months (Emanual, et al, 2006, raised plasma nerve growth factor levels associated with early-stage romantic love). Also, Marazziti, et al, in their publication in 1999 called 'Alteration of the platelet serotonin transporter in romantic love', and found that the most intense effects of romantic love lasts about twelve to eighteen months. The novelty wears off after a while, so it is important that you keep it hot; very important. Cooking in nothing but an apron and heels won't go amiss.

Seduction

The Oxford Dictionary's definition of seduction is: *entice into sexual activity*. The word "entice" means to attract or to tempt. What are your skills like? Are you any good at foreplay? Do you know what turns your man/link on? Not every man is the same. Some men like their nipples being licked/sucked; some men abhor it. The art of seduction, the art of being sexy, is a tool which shouldn't be taken for granted. If you haven't got a clue how to seduce, if you don't have the skills to make a man hard like freezer meat without touching him, feel free to go to Secrets or Spearmint rhino and see how the women there do it. It's not a joke when some men say they are in love with a stripper. The art of seduction is powerful. If you realise you are having problems when it comes to being intimate with a man, try picking up a book on tantric sex or surfing the net for some information. If you can no longer arouse your partner, there is no need to ask **Bobby**, just know **Houston** we have problems.

As silly as this may sound, food is a very good form of seducing a man into your lair—yes, food. They are not far off when they say that "food is the way to a man's heart". Let's not forget in the primitive times it wasn't love that led a man into the sheltering habitat of a woman. It was her shelter and food that allured man. Even with our closest relatives in the mammalian kingdom being the chimps (and bonobos), they use a similar technique in attracting male chimps. The method is known as 'sex for meat'. Scientists have found that the bartering of meat for sex has been taking place for long periods of time. It has formed part of a social fabric amongst a troop of wild chimps in the Tai National park in the Cote d'Ivore. If your man can't be lured into your fortress with food nor sex—babes, just call it a day. Move on. It is clear he is not into you. Don't allow your pride to kick in and kick you up the butt. Most men do not need to be emotionally attached to a woman to have sex with one, so if you find a man is not forthcoming when it comes to sex—seriously, just leave it. If you cooked him a gourmet meal, flung on some lingerie/killer heels, done a lap dance for him, and his man hasn't risen to attention. I feel sorry for you, I really do—just call it quits, babes.

No Need To Wash Your Mouth Out With Soap, I Love Your Filthy Mouth

You're so use to running your mouth when you're arguing, why is it now in the bedroom you're mute like pause? You better open your mouth and tell me how it is feeling, tell me you can feel it in your stomach, tell me it feels like I am pushing your organs up. However, if when he puts it in and it feels like a tampon, as in you can't feel anything, don't lie. Faking good sex will never make a man improve—since when has faking an orgasm made his techniques any better? It's okay, I can wait. Most of us men love the filth talk—oh, yes we do. Call me big daddy Kane, call me Bruce Banner, call me Sir Vix because I go that deep. Yes, be vocal in the bedroom. Talk to me mami, I'm your papi. Let him know when you're about to cum like the Dunns River. Men love being complimented; we do, especially when it comes to sex. I, for one, hate when a woman is not vocal—and the men I've asked have said the same thing. Feel free to call your man names, just not your ex's or another man's. So yes, speak up in the bedroom, don't feel shy; if the sex is good let him know it's good; if it's wack, let him know afterwards—and I am being serious. If the sex is no good, it's better you tell him so he can try and improve. Faking it will not make him any better.

Turn The Lights Off, Babe

Are you sexually confident? I mean, are you happy with your body? If you aren't, you may find that he may sense this. When a woman always want the lights turned off, always wants to have sex under the covers, some men may be put off. A woman who is happy with her body, it will more than likely show when it comes to foreplay and sex. Not being happy with your body can hinder one's sex life, it sure can. Women who are not sexually confident are less likely to want to do a sex tape with their man. (Let me slip this in quickly: under no circumstance should you do a sex tape with a man who isn't your partner, just know that all of his friends will view that video.)

If you don't like your body, then put your fitness first and head to Fitness First. It has been noted that when a person is happy with their body, they feel more esteemed about themselves. If you don't like your body, it is likely you're not going to feel at liberty in the bedroom, as you're going to feel self-conscious. And love is not blind, if your partner met you a size ten and you're now a size eighteen, you don't want what happened to Jill Scott in 'Why did I get married?' to happen to you. A word is enough for the wise.

"I must be honest with you, babe, I love to watch the faces that you make, but when I'm behind you holding your hips and you close your eyes and bite your lips, I can't see you, so might I suggest a change."—Neyo, Mirror.

Communication Is The Key

Ultimately, good sex revolves around communication. It's imperative that the two of you talk about sex, so you know one's likes and dislikes. It's important to know this, so you know what makes your partner's eyes roll to the back of their head and not roll their eyes at you. As a woman it's important to know whether or not you're pleasuring your man. Don't just assume that your sex is the bomb because you're a terrorist in your relationship. Spend time talking to each other, spend time exploring what he likes. Don't be afraid to ask; if you don't ask, you will never know.

However, with all forms of pleasure that one may ask for when it comes to sex, one has to ask themself: will this act harm their body? Your partner may want you to perform a sexual act, but if this act can harm your body then you have to think twice before allowing him to perform it. Many sexual activities can be psychologically or physically dangerous—or at least risky. Anal, for instance, can damage the tissues in one's anus and if that happens you're in deep shit—literally. So, yes, before you make an ass of yourself and decide to pleasure one's partner, think to yourself whether or not this act is risky and can cause future damage. Might I add it has been said that semen can reduce breast cancer by forty percent, so, ermmm, yeah, feel free to swallow what is on the menu—many thanks, amen, cheers. Oh, and might I add it contains protein, enzymes and sugar (mainly fructose) and the average ejaculation, which is one teaspoon, contains between five to twenty-five calories.

When a man putting his penis inside your vagina becomes sensually boring as a handshake, it no longer becomes sexually pleasurable for him; it now becomes simply sexual activity. There is a distinct difference between the two; as BT says: *it's good to talk*. Communicate with him to ensure your sex doesn't become as sensually boring as a shake of hands.

If you're looking for a man to complete you,
you've missed the whole point.

Can A Man And Woman Be Platonic Friends?

"Everything in the world is about sex except sex.
Sex is about power."

—*Oscar Wilde*

The word platonic was brought about by a philosopher called Plato. Platonic is an emotion/feeling towards someone that is non-sexual, as in the person has no sexual desires towards that individual—which, in turn, means one has no lustful thoughts for that person.

Lust, according to the Oxford Dictionary is:

- A strong sexual desire: *he knew that his lust for her had returned*
- A passionate desire for something: *a lust for power*
- Have strong sexual desire for someone: *he really lusted after me in those days*

Yes, they can be platonic friends, they sure can. It is possible for two people not to lust after each other as long as one deems the other party minging. The only way two people who are of the opposite sex can be platonic friends is if one of the parties has written the other person off in their head. For instance, a woman may find me attractive, she may think I'm the boom diggy, but then she discovers I have two kids (Disclaimer: The only **BMs** I deal with are **German vehicles, 6s** preferably), which may be a deal breaker for her, so therefore she can be my friend as she has no interest in me.

118

Now, where the problem lies, is that I may fancy her and if that be so, the advice I give her as a 'friend' may be warped, for the fact that I like her, which means any advice she requires about men, I will make sure I get my **square-chicken** on and **cockblock** nicely. If I, as a man, fancy you, why am I going to lead you into the arms of another man? My name is not Dillon McSweeney.

It is an innate propensity that man and woman come together for mating purposes; it is natural for a man to fancy a woman and vice versa. It's society, morals and ethics that has got some people curbing these sexual desires. The sex urge is enough to ensure that man and woman meet for the reproduction of the species. This instinct operated way before man experienced love, devotion and marital loyalty.

If you look at the female or male friends around you, the only reason why you're friends is probably because you don't deem them sexually attractive; they are butters, they look like they are stuck in evolution, or look like a baboon's bottom. It is innate for two people who are attracted to each other to want to mate. It is natural. The only reason why the two of them wouldn't is because of negating circumstances.

A woman may find a man attractive, but may not go there simply for the fact that he is broke or he is not on the same financial bracket as she is, so she refuses to unevenly yolk herself. However, the sexual attraction will still be present, so one can say she has him on layaway. Some would call it a dick in a jar, just waiting to be cracked open.

I, as a man, can tell you this for free. I have some females in my life that I consider my friend—not associate, friend. There are some I wouldn't sleep with, and the only reason I wouldn't is because I don't deem them good-looking, or they themselves have written me off. Either they don't think they could cope with me being their man or they know my thoughts on dating women with kids or they simply don't find me desirable. If two people find each other attractive there has to be a reason why they won't sleep with each other. If you're my friend and I find you pretty or sexy, just know that I will slip it in, if I was given the chance, YES I WOULD. *Man would penetrate.* I would put my magic wand inside your circus and begin performing tricks. Friends, my ass, if I find you attractive and I don't deem you to be broken, as in damaged goods, I will pierce. The only empathy I hold are for women who are hurting; other than that, I will sex you up, you better believe that. It's nothing long; in fact, it *is* long, long like a **ruler**, just thought I'd **straighten things out**. Ladies, I can tell you this for free—most testosterone-filled men around you, who fancy you, would likely slip it in if you gave them the chance. Don't be fooled—if you're their **type**, they will press those **keys**, no locksmith.

I remember one time I changed my relationship status on facebook to 'in a relationship'—the way my inbox got battered. It was hilarious. Couple girls were like "you're kidding, right?" Girls who I assumed were just friends, were like "What's going on 'ere?" Two girls deleted me, assuming it was true, so I guess they didn't want to see my face anymore. A lot of females will be nice to you, even help you with things; these things, at times, are in aid of trying to get you to like them. When a woman is helpful and puts herself out for me, I am grateful, but in the back of my mind I'm thinking: *are you this helpful to everyone? Or is it because you want the ting?* People are not generally nice for no reason. Yes, some folks are genuine, but we live in a world of Mr and Mrs Intentional. Hi, Nato.

There have been a couple girls who I have had around me who have fallen back (like Neyo's hairline) when they realised I wasn't interested in them.

There is one girl I know who fancies the pants off one guy, but he made the mistake of telling her that he has hit a woman before—that automatically put him in the friend zone. He got relegated nicely. Do you catch my drift? For two people to be friends there has to be something that works against them doing the dirty. For a woman to be a man's friend who she fancies, there has to be something blocking them from doing the *ting*. If not, they will at some point plank on each other.

There's Nothing Wrong With My Partner's Best Friend Being Of The Opposite Sex

You know your partner's type, right? If he/she is your partner's type, it is in your best interest to severe that relationship, even if it's for your own peace of mind. You know me; I say it as it is. Yeah, I'm **dark skinned** but I have **mixed race** vision. I see things as **black** and **white**. The more you spend time with somebody, the more you become fond of them; all it takes is that one night and it's tick-tick boom-boom pow. He may strike his match on her box and 'lighter' up. Attraction is attraction, you can't deny it. I know of women who have slept with their best friend's man. Yes, I kid you not. From when she fancies your man, she might go there. It's attraction. I have slept with friends of friends in the past. When a girl finds you attractive, it will take a lot to curb her sexual desires. This "men and women can be friends" thing is a myth as far as I am concerned. It only really works if both parties find each other unattractive; other than that, I am sorry, it is a lie, a big fat juicy one. My girl will not be having a close male friend that looks like me. Hell to the udder tucking no. So when she needs someone to talk to, she can go to his house, put her head on his shoulders, then end up putting her legs over his shoulders. I'm okay, thanks. I may be special but I am not special needs. I know what most men are like: sex is on the front, back and behind of their mind. In my hay day, I was that crying shoulder. First you start patting her head, telling her it will be all right, then you start rubbing her shoulders which ends up turning into a massage. She then looks you in the eye and gives you puppy eyes and then **boom-boom pow** she's riding my **black-eyed** pod of **peas**. Not every woman will fall for these antics, but one has to be careful. Intimate situations may lead to intimacy.

Why You Vex, Andre? I Only Gave Him My Pin. He's Not a Fraudster

Giving a man your pin, is like locking your front door but leaving your windows open. Please don't fool yourself. Unless you're exchanging contact details for business purposes, let's be serious. He has not taken your pin to be friends with you, let's not be naive. That's how some of you girls believe a man when he says he won't come inside of you, and then he arrives and parks his mandem in your chambers—now your eggs have to 'semen'. I come to you in the name of "Ramamandeep", unless it's for networking purposes, as in business, he is not taking your number to be your friend—and even if it *is* for business, if you are his type he will most likely want to slip it in. However, a businessman who puts money before women will seal the business deal first and then do the deed. Not every man is controlled by his penis. Some have learned that you can't chase money and chase women at the same time; one will get away. There are women around me who I deem attractive, but I won't sleep with them because I need them. I know if we sex, it may fark things up. Now this is the other side of the matter. When money is involved some men who are serious about their **cheddar** have **matured** so they won't go there; they are **greater** than that. Once again, there is something stopping them from doing the do. Unless it is for networking purposes under no circumstances should a man or woman be giving their pin or number out. And the way things are going with social networks, adding someone on twitter is just as bad. Some men are like a bureau de change, they will convert your pin into a pound (beat). A good strike-her has the ability to convert from almost anything. Once the contact is made, it is made.

Why You Vex, Lisa? It Was Just A Dance

Just a dance? Hmmmmmm, just a dance, yeah? Okay. I don't know about you but I don't dance with people that I deem to be unattractive—nope, sorry. If I ever caught my girl dancing with some dude in a club, I would tear off her eyebrow. I have seen women dismiss a man because he favoured Mark Morrison. Maybe in a Kizomba class or a Salsa class you may dance with someone you don't deem attractive but not in an 'Urban' rave. Nope, I am sorry, how can you have a man and be allowing a next man to rub his wand on your bum? Let's be real. You might as well say you're having dry sex. You think I could walk into a place and see my missus skinning out to Dumpa Truck on someone she deems as her friend. Does she want to lose a breast? I will call a dumper truck to come to the house and come and collect her stuff. Pause and ask yourself this: when was the last time you danced with someone you deemed unattractive? If you did, the situation was an anomaly or was out of pity.

It is foul play to allow another man to be scrubbing you when you have a man. P45s will be issued on site. The amount of times I have been out and I have been scrubbing a woman and then I discover she has a man, I'm like *"What the fark?"* How are you letting me do this to you and you have a man?

And, lads, let's be real, we do not approach girls to dance if we think they look precious (pun intended).

So What Are You Saying, Dear Rob? Are You Saying Men And Women Can't Be Platonic Friends? Say It Ain't So

With the definition of what a platonic friend is—yes, they can be platonic friends, as long as they do not find each other attractive and there are reasons why they have written that individual off. With men and women it differs. One of the main reasons why a man wouldn't bone a woman is because he needs her for business purposes. I know a few men who run businesses who have hot members of staff; they won't go there as they don't want it to interfere with their projects. I know men who are landlords who have hot tenants as friends; they won't sleep with them because they don't want them one day trying to default payment. Once one becomes familiar, it often breeds contempt. Obviously there are men out there who are faithful, so wouldn't sleep with a friend because of this. However, if that girl put it on him, I don't know what the outcome would be. It's very hard for a man to refuse sex on a plate, very hard; many men have refused it but it will be extremely difficult if you find that woman attractive.

Even when it comes to giving advice in regards to helping a friend out, if I fancy you, I am not going to give you advice that will favour the guy that likes you, hell no. I will sabotage. That's why I always say that women should seek advice from men who are genuinely platonic and have your best interest at heart. If the said dude fancies you, his opinion will most likely be biased.

If you want a yes or a no answer for "can men and women be friends?" I will categorically say NO, as the mating instinct is the reason why male and female species come together. It is an innate propensity. If you are attracted to someone you can only curb it for so long.

Think of the hot friends you have around you; there are reasons why you haven't jumped them but that doesn't stop you having lustful thoughts. It only takes a glitch in the **matrix**, for a man to forget his morals and become a **freeman**.

Might I add, most of the sexual encounters that are acted upon happen in the work place; it's an easy excuse for one another to be talking. We all remember what happened with Bill Clinton and Monica Lewinsky. Let's just say she knew how to make the president stand to attention.

Oh, and one of the best ways to let a friend know that you're not interested in them is by asking them for advice on other members of the opposite sex. That will soon put a nail in the coffin.

If you're looking for a man to complete you,
you've missed the whole point.

Why Do Some Men Cheat? What Is The Meaning?

"Young men want to be faithful, and are not; old men want to be faithless, and cannot."

—*Oscar Wilde*

Break it down for us Rob, break it down for us.

Well well well, if you want the honest truth, we do it because we want to. Yes, *want to*. There doesn't need to be some psychoanalytic analysis as to why men cheat; we do it because we want to. Some of us just love to stroke as many cats as possible. Humans beings are not designed to be monogamous; they are not. In the mammalian kingdom monogamy is rare (and for those of you who do not know . . . yes, we as humans are mammals). It's so rare that it is one of the most unusual behaviours in biology. Monogamy is cultural and societal; artificial and unnatural to the evolutionary human. Yes, I said unnatural. Pick up a book on anthropology and it will explain how unnatural it is. However, in saying that, monogamy is and always has been the idealistic goal of human sex evolution. But it works a heavy strain on humans/men who can't achieve this. As stated, monogamy is not natural but it *is* needed for the furthering and maintenance of social civilisation.

Monogamy is control; it is great for those who want this desirable state, but it often works a biologic strain on those who are not so auspicious. But in spite of the effect on the individual, monogamy is unequivocally best for the children.

The earliest monogamy was because of the force of circumstances, scarcity. A shortage in resources led man into this state. However, monogamy is the benchmark which measures the progress of social civilisation as ascertained from purely biologic evolution. Monogamy is not fundamentally biologic or natural, but it *is* indispensable to the immediate continuance and further development of social civilisation. It contributes to a delicacy of sentiment, a purification of moral character, and a spiritual growth which I believe is wholly not viable in polygamy.

I don't believe a woman in this day and age can ever become an ideal mother when she is all the while obliged to commit in rivalry for her husband's care. However, polygamy is to do with having multiple wives. A man being promiscuous and dipping out once in a while isn't; let's not confuse the two.

I hear you screaming from the rooftops: *but why is it that so many women can curb their desire but men can't, why is this?*

"The fact that males produce numerous and cheap sperm, while females produce few and expensive eggs, has two important consequences. First . . . a male may potentially fertilize many females, whereas females are limited by the number of eggs, and thus offspring, that they can produce and raise. Males, thus, will benefit by trying to fertilize as many females as possible, and will compete for access to reproductive females. In contrast, females will benefit by mating with the best mate possible."—Mills et al, 2010: 544

This is one reason why women can curb their sexual desires; females need to ensure that they mate with the best males possible as to ensure better survival for their offspring in case of pregnancy.

Women, because of physical and emotional attachment to her children, are reliant on the cooperation of a man and it's this that pushes her into the sheltering protection of fidelity. Please understand that no direct biological urge led men into monogamy—much less held him in. It was not love that made monogamy alluring to man; it was food hunger which first attracted savage man to woman and the primitive shelter shared by her children. Bear this is mind. It wasn't love that led men to want to cleave unto the bosom of a woman, it wasn't. A man can hammer as many nails as he wants with his instrument and literally walk away; a woman can't. As men, we can do an Osama bin hiding and never be seen again. As a woman you are left with the responsibility. Also, if you slept with Tom, Kunle and Percy during the period when you can conceive, it is likely you'd become a victim of the Jeremy Kyle show. These things alone force a woman to curb her sexual desires. A man can nut as much as he wants; he has no physical ties to a child, whereas you as a woman are tied to that child through your umbilical cord. It's a woman's instinct to love and care for her child that leads her into monogamy. Not saying that a man doesn't want to but a woman's maternal instinct tends to make her opposed to cheating, coupled with the double standard that society has when it comes to men and women sleeping around.

One also has to remember that most women connect emotionally when it comes to sex; many a man don't. Most men do not necessarily attach emotions with sex; they can simply slip their man down the cat's throat and be gone and never think of her again. Whereas most women need to form some sort of an emotional tie before spreading her legs like gossip. One thing a lot of people seem to forget is that men and women are two different species; we are not the same. You have these weird things on your chest. I think they're called breasts. They even produce milk. How weird. I kid, I kid. I would like to add, research suggests that there are two-hundred and thirty-seven reasons as to why one has sex, which fall into thirteen subcategories (Meeston and Buss, 2007). These include:

Physical: stress reduction, pleasure, desirability, experience seeking.

Goal Attainment: resources, social status, revenge, utilitarian.

Emotional: love/commitment and expression.

Insecurity: self-esteem boost, duty/pressure, mate guarding.

As you can see there are numerous reasons why a human/man may need to go and stroke a stray cat.

Enough Of The Anthropology Jargon, Rob, Why Do Some Of These Men Like To Dip Their Nuggets Into So Many Different Sauces?

Whether you want to call it adultery, infidelity, or cheating, men have been doing this for a long time; it is not a new phenomenon. It isn't a new craze like this epidemic that has plagued women and has got them shaving the side of their heads off, looking like the Kellogg's rooster chicken.

Let me first off start by saying that unlike most women, men generally do not need a reason to cheat. Even though I will highlight the reasons why some men may stray, even if you're the best woman you could ever be, even if you take a penis and two balls in your mouth at the same time, as well as prepare some peppered steak, pounded yam and some egusi, your man may still cheat. Yes, he could, so don't go slitting your wrist, doing a Britney Spears and start shaving your hair off, especially if you can honestly say to yourself that you are a good woman. Most men do not need a reason to cheat. However, I will break down some of the reasons as to why some may.

Oh, and might I add, Abraham, Jacob, Moses and David all had multiple wives/concubines. So for those who try to use the G-d of the Bible to advocate monogamy/fidelity—think again. In 2 Samuel 12 vs. 8 it states "I gave your master's house to you, and your master's wives into your arms. I gave you all Israel and Judah. And if all this had been too little, I would have given you even more." It's if you want to be a deacon/elder that you are only allowed to have one wife, as it states in 1 Timothy 3 2: "A bishop then must be blameless, the husband of one wife, vigilant, sober, of good behaviour, given to hospitality, apt to teach." The only reason why one can't have multiple wives in the west is because the state is against it. Not that one would want multiply wives anyway; one woman's headache is enough. Just wanted to clear that up. If G-d of the Bible was against men having more than one woman why would he give David multiple wives and then say he would have given him more if they weren't enough? If the Bible is anything to go by men have had a thing for having a harem of women for a long time. However, I believe monogamy is best for the family. But do understand that to someone who has just turned vegetarian the smell of meat will still be alluring to them.

Your Belly And Breast Have Started Competing For Who Is The Bustier Challenge

He met you as a size 10 and now you're a size 18. As much as one may want to use the excuse of pregnancy, there are many women out there who have had kids and shed the weight—many; that is not really a plausible excuse. For a lot of women it's simply the fact that she got comfortable. Got into the routine of having a man and decided to eat, eat and eat until her chin gave birth to another one. If you ladies haven't noticed, us men are visual creatures; love may be blind but G-d gave us hands to feel. Yes, it may sound shallow that a man cheats because of this, but if your man no longer finds you attractive, he may go and do the do elsewhere. It might even be for medical reasons as to why one has put on the weight—yes, it sounds cold-hearted but some may cheat for these reasons.

Lack Of Sex

Not that it is written in stone anywhere that a woman must provide access to her man whenever he wants to enter, but withholding sex from your man is one reason why he may stray. Errmmm, if you, as his woman, is not giving him sex, where do you want him to get it from? Sorry, babes, I only mass debate in group discussions. It has been said that testosterone,

one of the hormones responsible for the sex drive, is 20-40% higher in men than in women. It's not always the case, but men do tend to have a higher sex drive than women. If your man wants to enter your gates every day and you only want to have sex once a week, this is going to cause a huge problem (pun not intended). Women tend to need to feel close to their partner, emotionally, to desire sex, whereas men tend to need physical intimacy before they invest a great deal of energy into their relationship. We are wired different. Withholding sex from a man could make him feel like you no longer desire him; so he goes elsewhere to fulfil that emptiness. When a man needs to buss juice, he needs to buss juice. Before couples get together it is imperative that one discusses this. The best way to jump start your sex drive is to just do it. One thing most men can't do is go back sexually; if his ex was a freak and wanted sex all the time and you on the other hand just want it here and there, you two will eventually hit a brick wall.

The Fact He Hasn't Peaked Yet

Yes, I believe every man has to get to that stage where he has peaked; the point where he no longer feels the need to flatter his ego. A man needs to sow his royal oats; I believe it is imperative that a man gets it out of his system. This may involve going on boys' holidays; for some men they've fantasised about having a threesome; for some it may be having one night stands. Most men are as faithful as their options. A man could be dating a girl, all is going well, and then he falls into money. All of a sudden his options have expanded. His Clio has changed into a **Range** and now all the girls are being a good **sport**. He is now in **vogue**. He has finally peaked. His girl may be in trouble as he can now do the things he wasn't able to do before. Prior to '06 I was so broke I couldn't afford to cash a reality cheque; I knew it would bounce. Yeah, I got girls, but it was a struggle as I couldn't take them out on dates and most girls would require pussy payments before letting you stroke the cat—at that point I put girls on hold. '06 came and I started making money—oh, sweet Jesus, the way my life changed. I could do things with girls that I had dreamed of doing. Between '06 and '09 I peaked. I sowed my royal oats. I believe it's something most men need to do before settling. A lot of men peak late and these are the ones who you tend to find 'beating' up the place when they have girlfriends. When a man no longer needs to flatter his ego and realises that his crown jewels are only meant to be put on his queen's head, that's when he will try and stop. Other than that: happy relations.

Non-Stop Nagging

No matter how much money a man makes, if he can't find peace of mind at home, it is pointless. Is him leaving the toilet seat up that important for you to create an argument over it? There's kids dying in Iraq and Afghanistan every day, and *this* is what you find important to argue about? Just put the seat down and done. It's not everything that you need to moan about. Keep moaning and you may just moan your man into the arms of another chick; that side chick, the one who gives him no grief when he goes to her house. She understands that he likes to watch football and sets reminders on the Sky box, so that when they're watching a programme it flashes up. She understands that arguing about the small things is not important. Longevity of relationships are based on how well two individuals can deal with conflict. A nagging woman will keep a man away from home in most cases.

Feel free to complain about the fact he likes sports, just know that the skinny *bish* at his workplace has bought him tickets to the FA Cup final and you aren't invited.

Loss Of Sex Appeal

Sorry to say this, but after years of stroking the same cat, some men get bored—especially when every night you come into the bedroom with your doorag on, looking like Mark Morrison, with your head top smelling like sulphur 8. What is the meaning? As a woman you have to learn to keep it hot in the house. As you know, we are visual creatures. Fling on some heels once in a while and cook in nothing but your apron. It is imperative that you keep your man stimulated. Send him racy messages in the day, make him want to come home and attend to kitty. For most women sex is emotional, for most men it's just a physical act. As much as he may love you, our hearts are not necessarily connected to our penis. I would be bold enough to say it isn't. We need to be stimulated. Have you lost the art of seduction? If so, head over to your local strip club and see how these bad *bishes* do their thang. When a man has lost his **sex drive** for you, it is very hard to get that **engine running** again. You have to keep it **hot**, or don't be surprised when his name changes to **Luke Warm**.

Lack Of Attention

Are you one of these new age women who work around the clock, going to a meeting here, a meeting there? When you come home you're tired; so tired that you rarely cook anymore. Have you stopped telling your man how great he is? That's if he is; there is no point lying. Some men crave the attention of their woman. Have you become so busy that you no longer have time to spend with your man? If you watched 'Why did I get married?' you will remember Tyler Perry's wife in the film. She was forever on her phone, even when they went on vacation, she was constantly working. Is this you? Has your career taken over your life? As much as some men may try and play Mr Brawn, some of us do have feelings, man. A lack of attention and appreciation could easily drive your man into arms of another woman. But in saying that, so could too much, one has to find the balance.

These are just some of the things that may lead your man to cheat but as stated earlier you could be the best woman and he may still cheat. Men and women are different; where most women may need a reason to cheat, most men don't.

Yes, there are faithful men out there, there sure is, not all men cheat. However, there are some reasons as to why some men don't cheat. Earlier I mentioned that most men are as faithful as their options. I will break this down for you now.

I will start by saying this: a drowning man will clutch onto anything to save himself. If a man is on his face, broke like a clock with no hands and lives in your house, his options are very limited. First of all, he has no money to entertain women; second, he lives in your house. Now, in this day and age, a man will have to take a woman out once or twice before he can get to stroke Sheba. If he can't make the payments to get to the cat, he will be left with Nathan in most circumstances. A man who lives with you and is reliant on you in most circumstances won't cheat because he knows that if he does he may be put out on the street like Mike Skinner. He needs you more than you need him. Relationships are a game of leverages; a game of who needs who more. Right now he needs you, so therefore it's in his best interest to be on his best behaviour.

I am not saying that it's only when a man is in dire straits that he won't cheat, but these circumstances seem to be the most common in my findings. A lot of men tend not to cheat when they have kids with a woman because they know if they do and get caught that she might jump on a plane to New Zealand and he may never see his kids again. Then you have the other bunch of men who have never been the promiscuous type—the Dillons, the good guys. The guys that tend to get overlooked because they don't look fly like a zipper. They get overlooked because they have no 'swag'. We also have the guys who are simply tired of sleeping around and sex literally bores them. Yes, bores them, they've conquered so much pussy that branching out doesn't entice them anymore.

There are many reasons why a man will cheat and not cheat; there are men out there who won't cheat simply for the fact their missus knows too much dirt about them, hence the phrase 'it may be cheaper to keep-her'. When your woman knows all about your dodgy dealings as a man, it is in your best interest to keep her sweet rather than sour.

Many like to assume that a man cheating boils down to sexual dissatisfaction; as stated, you could be the head mistress—most men like a woman who isn't ghetto but knows her way around the hood—and it will still happen. I would like to say it more boils down to a bit of narcissism and low contentiousness. Once the sex novelty has worn off, most men will cheat regardless. Once that lustful drive that once lured him into your lair has diminished, his fidelity towards you will likely finish.

Even if you, as a woman, are doing wrong, it's for him to come and speak to you so that you can make amends; him cheating on you is not an excuse. It is not. The reason you are together is under the premise that both parties are faithful. But understand it's not him, it's biology. Truth be told, I am not going to say that a woman should accept that most men will cheat, but it is not a new phenomenon. Women tend to cheat emotionally and men tend to cheat physically. A man cheating on you does not mean he doesn't love you. That same dude will more than likely take a bullet for you. Erections do not have emotions. As Mr west said: "I suppose you was told by those hos that I was cheating, but my heart don't gots nothing to do with my penis." A man can be faithful, it *is* possible; however, if you're the type that withholds sex from your man: GOOD LUCK.

If you're looking for a man to complete you,
you've missed the whole point.

How To Know If You Might Be In A Relationship With A Single Man

"Woman wants monogamy; Man delights in novelty."

—Dorothy Parker

Public Signs

Why oh why is your man going to a Trey Songz concert? Does he wear skinny jeans and gladiator sandals? If not, what is his reason for going there? He is most likely going to draw girls—and please believe me he isn't an artist.

Why is that whenever you and him go out he always takes you to a place that ends in shire (for those who live in London)? Shropshire, Cambridgeshire, etc. Why doesn't he take you to the places that he frequents? I'll tell you why: he doesn't want to get caught out, so he takes you to obscure locations, so he doesn't get spotted like the last days of a period. Ask him to take you to the places he often goes. Why is it good for him and not good for the both of you?

So you walked into a bar and all of a sudden he says he doesn't want to drink here anymore and makes a quick beeline for the door and you know he hasn't parked illegally. He has more than likely seen a **link** in there and doesn't want you to break the **chain**.

If a guy is really slick, what he would do is park up, go in the restaurant/bar first and check if the coast is clear. Watch out for those manoeuvres.

So your man went on a boys' holiday. What do you think he went to do in Miami? Chill with the lads, yeah? Please don't fool yourself. Yes, there are guys who may go there and want to sunbathe with some hot segsee Brazilian mamis, but that is the odd one in a million, and I ain't talking about Aaliyah. Where are the pictures? Guys are so bait. How come he has no pictures with any girls? That alone is suspect. Surely he mingled with girls. But the guilt won't let him show you any pictures with females.

Six months in and you haven't met his mum and she lives in the country. Why? Why? Why is he hiding you from his family? Why? I tell you why; he most probably has another girlfriend or has more kids that he hasn't told you of. It is imperative that if you claim to have a man that you meet his family. Many men have girlfriends and they know their mum won't stand for the cheating so they keep you away; in saying that, some mums are on the payroll and will lie for their sons so be careful.

You and he are in the same rave and he didn't invite you to a party where he is/was—some of his concubines are most probably loitering around and he doesn't want the commotion. A man who isn't cheating will feel no way having you in his arms in public.

So it was his birthday, he invited you to the dinner, but never invited you to the after party, why? Why couldn't you go to the rave? Well, he has told his side chick to go there; he most probably lied to her and told her that was all he would be doing.

If you never got the birthday sex on his birthday, he more than likely gave it to somebody else. Don't be upset. Jesus died for you.

So you went to the cinema to watch a film and while watching the film, at all the scary and funny parts he never flinched. He seemed to know the story line. Yep, he has most likely watched the film already. That's why the cashier winked at him.

So he has gone on a business trip: to where? This is the easiest excuse to cheat, especially when one is self-employed.

Why do you allow your man to go raving continuously? Why does he go raving week in week out? What is in the club for him? If he is not a DJ or a promoter (and even those guys tend to be the worst) why is he out all the time? He is going to draw numbers. Plain and simple. Men generally aren't getting dressed, spunking dough, just to go home. I am sorry, he is not. He goes there to draw. Since I've stopped battering the rave scene my sex life has been shit, as I have no links.

The Curves On Her Waist Created A Storm, So I Had To Blackberry Her

Why does your man have a BlackBerry and you are not on it? Do you just enjoy mugging yourself? Do you enjoy being special . . .? *Needs*, that is. Why won't he add you to his BlackBerry? Let me guess. He doesn't want you seeing his updates of where he might be going—and, also, you can't tell whether or not he has read your message.

Between 9-11pm is what is known as linking hours. Let's say you've gone to work, finished at 5pm, got home for 6pm, freshened up by 7pm. If she is making her way to his he will *deffo* be with her between those hours. If you think back, it is usually between 9 and 11pm he has difficulty answering his phone.

You see that name that is saved in his phone as Angelo . . .? Take that O and replace it with an A. Yes, don't for one second get it twisted; guys will save a girl's name in their phone under a man's name so that if she rings when he is with you he can say that it's his mate.

That folder in his phone that says "create folder"—he renamed it that. Open it and you will see what he has inside that folder. That's where all the shit is hidden.

Why does your man have a pin to his phone and he refuses to tell you? What is he hiding? Okay, what about whenever you want to use his phone, you have to hand it to him for him to put his pin in and hand it back to you . . .? Do you enjoy being special . . .? *Needs*, that is. Come on, it's only a man who has *su'in* to hide that will not want you having his pin.

Why is that when you rang his phone, it said "the mobile phone is unavailable"? That is because he more than likely took out the battery, so it would say that. Watch out for those tricks there.

So you rang him and he is texting you back. Why is he texting you back? You know his work pattern and he ain't at work. He is most probably with a link so he can't pick up. If he calls you back the following day, you don't need the cooker to tell you what time it is.

Why is it that his phone never rings when he is with you, but he always seems to be on it when you aren't around? Yeah, he has diverted his calls to voicemail, or even better: put it on flight mode. Why ain't it ringing?

Watch out for guys who always call on private number; that is the number he doesn't want you to have; understand you're just that sweet corn, the side chick; don't be upset, Horus died for you. Oh, and so did Mithra. Oh, and so did Tamos. These new gadgets can ring themselves now; don't fall for that "I've got to go, my mate is in trouble" line. He could be using that to go and link another chick.

So his phone rang and it said 'Sarah'. What he did, is that he pressed the silent button, put the phone to his ear and started talking to himself. So all this time when he was saying he was at his girl's house, he was talking to no one and you got all happy that he told a girl he was at his girl's, paahahahahahahahaaa.

Looking through his phone and you can't find any girls names? Put a full stop first and then you will see them, e.g. Angela. Sheila . . . Do you catch my drift?

Watch out for the guys who will claim they are going raving with the lads, but go to a girl's house and then come back at about four in the morning. If he is leaving your house at 4am, he is most likely going to his girl's. What these guys will do, is post up old pictures on their BB, professing to be in a club.

Social Networks

Why does your man have a Facebook and you are not on it? That there is a complete and utter *muggins*, of the highest calibre. Social networks are the easiest devices to catch a swine out; from tagged pictures to girls leaving comments on pictures.

Back in the day Dwayne could be any Dwayne. Now you can put a face to that mofo.

Why is it that he doesn't have a picture of you on his Facebook? Since when did a man want to hide a good thing? Since when? When a man has a good thing he shows it off. I guess you're just that best kept secret.

He has pictures with himself and other girls but not with you . . .? It's clear he doesn't want anyone knowing about you, so that no one inboxes him, asking who you are.

So he tells you he doesn't want a picture of you and him up on your Facebook. Why is that? What's wrong with that? What's the big deal?

Watch out for the guys with two Facebook accounts. Just because he has added you on one doesn't mean *nada*.

His House

You've come to his house and discovered a half bottle of Rosé in the fridge; most, if not all, bruddas don't drink Rosé in their house. That mofo drank that *ish* with some girl. All of them kind of fruity drinks like wine, he never drunk with the lads. Unless, once again, he wears skinny jeans and gladiators. Other than that, he was in the house with some next *bish*.

So you came round to watch a DVD and you suggest "Diary of a mad black woman" and he says, "We've watched that already, babes," and you fully well know you haven't. Just know he has watched it before, but with a next chick.

So you've come round to his and the place is extra spotless—I mean, cleaned behind the toaster—and you know how his flat usually looks. Even his Xbox pads are folded away. Just know his sister never came round. It was another chick who stayed round and tidied up, polished the TV and him.

Or, let's say you've gone in his draw and there were six condoms the last time you went in there, and now there are four—don't be stupid, he did *not* give them to his boy, he did not. He used them. Yes, he did. I don't care; please do not buy that line, let alone take it for free. And if he does claim he gave it to his friend, tell him to call the friend, right this minute, and make sure he doesn't send a text.

The way I got caught out with my ex was this: she rang me and said she left a pair of earrings at mine, but she hadn't. So, like a prick, I said: "Yeah, I've found them." This time the earrings weren't hers, they belonged to someone else. Checkmate. Grrrrrrrrrrrrrr.

Different colour hair. I learned from this. Only cheat on your missus with girls who have the same length and colour hair as her. A woman knows when she is looking at another *bishes* hair.

He changed his sheets and pillows just two days ago, why is he changing them again? Who has been squirting on the sheets? Who has left foundation on his pillow case?

Why does he have a key to your house and you don't have one to his? Stop mugging yourself off.

Understand this, men generally don't sleep at each other's houses randomly. Don't fall for that. If your man went out raving and never came home, he most likely slept at a chick's house. Yes, he did. I can't tell you the last time I slept at one of my male friends' house. We would rather go home, unless you're that nagging type . . . Yucky.

At Work

All of a sudden he has started making effort in the way he dresses at work. Why? What is there for him all of a sudden that he has now taken a different pride in his appearance?

You used to get an invite to the work dinners and parties, now you don't. He is most likely boning someone in the office and doesn't want to get caught out like Ghanaians with no passport on Boarder Force.

The moment you no longer get invited to his work functions, there is a reason. "I was working late, honey." Okay, but what 'figures' was he working late on?

His Car

So you've got to his car and the seat is pulled right to the front. What girl was in your car, pal?

You've got to his car and the back seat is reclined all the way. Yeah, he was smooching some chick and wound it back so he could do the do.

Shout out to the mandem who keep a spare pair of boxers in the gym bag in the boot. Can't be getting caught with the cum stains, can we?

Check the passenger visor; women tend to leave their foundation fingerprints on there.

Exhales

Ultimately, if your man is going to cheat there is nothing you can do about it. Do not pull your hair out and slit your wrists.

Not all men cheat, so don't think they all do. But I will say this: if you have been with your man five years plus and you have not caught him cheat, that is love right there. When a man loves you he will pull out all the stops to ensure he doesn't get caught. As crazy as it sounds, fidelity is not for every male. It is not natural. I often hear women saying that if a man can't be faithful he should stay single. Do you know how many of you would be single if that be the case?

Before you leave a man who cheats on you, and you have kids with him, you have to think to yourself: is he a good dad? Does he take care of the home? Is he a good partner?

There are different forms of cheating. If a man is beating the next door neighbour, it is clear he has no respect for you. If he is chopping someone in your work place, he clearly doesn't. Did you find condoms in his bin? He doesn't care. But if you found he was stroking a cat miles away, then you have to understand that he actually is trying to shield you from it.

Remember when you leave a man because of infidelity you have to ask yourself one question: who actually wins? If you move out with your kids and live in a hostel, eating noodles and ketchup, who wins?

A man can cheat on you and still love you; most men do not value sex. It is just sex. Most of us would stick our willies in a wet hoover if it would make us cum. It is just another extension of our body. Consider it a third arm. And yes, mine is as long as an arm.

I haven't mentioned everything, but the key in knowing if you might be in a relationship with a single man is simply having common sense. One thing you girls need to stop doing is calling a man on the phone when trying to catch him out. *STOP IT*. He can easily hang up and call a friend. Wait until he gets home and confront him. That way he can't hang up and try and make up a cock and bull story. Also, pour him a drink; if he is lying he will use the drink to bide time.

As stated previously, the act of sex does not negate the fact that he loves you; think about this before you start picking up your bags and doing a runner. That same man who cheats on you, would most likely take a bullet for you.

If you're looking for a man to complete you,
you've missed the whole point.

Having Two Black Eyes Is Not What Is Meant By Love Is Blind

"I prayed for twenty years to be freed as a slave but received
no answer until I prayed with my legs."
—*Frederick Douglass*

Domestic violence is something that is rife, but is something that seems to get swept under the rug like Brazilian hair when a date comes to your house and catches you off guard.

Here are some statistics for you, 1 in 4 women will be a victim of domestic violence in their lifetime and the majority of them on numerous occasions. One incident of domestic violence is reported to the police every minute. Yes, you're reading right, there is no need to adjust your reading glasses. Yes, one incident every minute. That is one thousand four hundred and forty incidences every day. Let's not forget that these are just the incidences that are reported; there are many women who just sit there and suffer in silence. On average, it is said that two women are killed a week by their current or former partner. That's just over one hundred women a year dying through domestic violence each year. (Stats acquired from the British Crime Survey).

What is domestic violence? Domestic violence is, as most know it, physical violence which may take place in an intimate or family type relationship. Now, it doesn't just stop there. Domestic violence can also be psychological.

Physical Abuse

This can involve slapping, pushing, kicking. Any form of pain inflicted on the body. Most times, it starts from a flick on the head. Most men who hit women tend to gauge whether they can or not. They start small and then get with the full blown attacks. Bunch of cowards. The day a man flicks you in your head, you bend his finger back and let him know it stops there. These poor excuses for men like to push boundaries. If you let them get away with a flick on the head, it is more than likely that he will get more advanced in his ways. He might even be cheeky enough to watch some wrestling programmes in front of you and then demonstrate what he has witnessed there on you. Don't have it. Don't stand for it. A man has no right to just start laying into you like you're some punching bag, no right. Don't allow him to convince you that it was you that head butted his fist. A lot of men have ways of manipulation. The moment you allow yourself to trip and fall victim to his cowardly ways, you're well and truly forked.

As a young boy I witnessed my mum go through domestic violence and it was not a pleasant sight. The trauma it put my mother through was enough to put her in a mental home. My asshole of a sperm donor father would perform all sorts of wrestling moves on my mum. The last straw was when he tried to strangle her with a telephone cable while she tried to call 999. What cowardice of a man? How dare I even use man and him in the same sentence—? What an oxymoron.

My mum let him back many times as she believed he would change; it has been proven that most men do not change. Don't for one second take the chance and believe the tears and gifts; return them back to sender. I come to you in the name of Roman Abramovich. As addictive as his manly wand may be, do not fall for his tricks. The moment a man lays hands on you, run like Forrest. Just keep running. In all my years on this earth I have never hit a woman, never. So when people say that these things can be passed down, there may be truth in it, but it never got passed down to me. Unless my life was in danger, and I mean, a woman had a knife to my throat or a hammer at my head, I see no reason why I must hit her. I am man enough to restrain her. But believe you me I'd shake the *ish* out a woman for hitting me. Might alter her DNA slightly. I kid, I kid, but you get my drift.

How many black eyes will you receive? How many times will you allow him to treat you like a happy slap victim? Is this life? To the point where you no longer need to buy eye shadow because the black eyes have rendered it useless. So many men hit women and it makes me sick. I don't care if she has provoked, I don't care. Why must one lash out? But I must say, ladies, if you hit a man first, you can't complain if he hits you back. No, I am not condoning a man hitting you, but if you punch a man and he snaps your jaw bone in one-thousand two hundred and thirty-four places, can you really complain? You can determine your actions but you can't determine another's *re*action.

Do not stay in a relationship where a man is hitting you, do not. That is not what is meant by tough love. His love should not be tough like that. That is not tough. Do not become another statistic, I come to you in the name of Krishna, Mithras, Jesus, Mohammed—whichever name or deity you are familiar with. I know in some religious texts it says the only ground for divorce is adultery, and if you divorce for any other reason, one can't remarry. Scrap that. Yes, I said scrap that. You shouldn't live the rest of your life like a victim. If the G-ds of religious texts are as loving and caring as they say they are, they will understand. Divorce that mofo if you are married to him. Don't allow such texts to hold you emotionally hostage. Maybe such behaviour was allowed then, but we're in the year 2000+ . . . no woman need stand for such treatment.

Psychological Abuse

Big sigh. This form of abuse can actually be deemed worse than the physical. They sort of go hand in hand. Psychological abuse is when you make someone subject to behaviour that is harmful to one's mind. Your man coming home and telling you that you're *craps*, that you're worthless. Telling you you're ugly, telling you that you look like you're stuck in evolution. These forms of abuse are the ones that tend to rob women of their confidence. Once you've lost your confidence, you're well and truly forked. Once you have lost your confidence, you lose your drive; you lose what you stand for. Some men use these methods to hold you hostage in a relationship. They tell you that you're craps, they tell you this in order to make you believe that they are doing you a favour by staying with you. They tell you these things to make you think that if you leave that nobody else would want you. But *he* wanted you, so surely he is not the only man that will. Do not allow a man to rob you of your confidence. Your confidence is so important. It is one thing that people with intuition can read when first meeting someone. Many women have given a *butters* man her number because he was confident; it's also confidence that has got many people the job that their qualifications/experience wouldn't have necessarily got them.

Psychological abuse is no joke; it's this that tends to render so many women stuck in cul de sac relationships. Once a man has been able to penetrate your equilibrium with such vitriol, you're in trouble, babes—serious trouble. Once he starts calling you names, shut it down like a Dell laptop and let him know that you may be short, but you will not stand for it. A man will treat you how you allow him to treat you. If you allow a man to treat you like craps, he will treat you like craps. We *mirror* you. A man should make you feel special like a bunch of kids on a blue bus. Not like craps. As stated earlier, a lot of men use these methods to try and break you down like drug dealers do with a box of food.

Signs He Might Be A Woman Beater

To be honest, this is really difficult to determine, as it has been said in many cases that he was *the most loving guy I have ever met.* He was so nice, etc., but then he turned out to be some monster. One thing I will say is watch out for men who like to blame you for everything; men who can't accept fault. Watch out for men who have anger issues in general. A man who finds himself punching doors and shouting at you may one day be that man who hits you. A man who says you shouldn't have made me mad, if not I wouldn't have punched through the door, that door may one day be your face. Watch out for signs of aggression. I know this may sound silly, but if possible, find out if he hit his previous girlfriend. A lot of women ask a man they newly meet if he has cheated before, but never seem to ask if he has beat before. I wouldn't advise a woman to date a man who has hit a woman before. I just wouldn't. Obviously, it depends on the circumstances, but as a yes or no, I would say no. People change, so it really is difficult to determine whether or not one can tell if a man will beat them or not.

As long as a man can blame his actions on something or someone else, he will most likely not seek help for what is clearly a case for anger management. A man blaming his anger issues on you is a straight red flag as far as I am concerned. Denial is not only a river that flows in Egypt; it flows through the veins of many.

Does he get angry about trivial matters? What is his reaction when you have an adverse opinion to his?

Watch out for men who try to alienate you from your friends and family so that you're solely dependent on him.

Look out for someone who wants to be with you all the time, even when you're with your family and friends. Look out for that man who needs to know where you are at all times and constantly turns up wherever you are; someone who wants to know who is on the phone whenever it rings. Basically, someone who wants to try and control you, someone who has obsessive-compulsive disorder.

All these things may give off some signals but aren't absolute.

Why Do Some Men Hit Women, Why Do Some Men Get A Kick Out Of It?

(Pun Intended)

Because they are cowards, because their brains were circumcised at birth, because they have anger management issues. Or maybe they were bullied in school by boys and now decide to vent their frustration out on women.

There are numerous reasons why.

I would like to use the word coward; any man who takes pleasure in hitting a woman is a sick, asinine degenerate. Unless a man is being attacked and his life is in danger, I see no reason why a man should hit a woman. And for those men reading this, we have a double standard in this world, we can sleep with as many women and tend not to get labelled, but when a woman does so, she is a ho. There are double standards whether we like it or not. Hitting a woman is cowardice. Yes, cowardice. Why not restrain her? Are you not man enough to restrain your woman? In saying that, if a woman spat on me or made me raise a child under the premise that it was mine and it wasn't, G-d help her.

A lot of men have used the excuse of *she provoked me* as to why he hit her. Now, ladies, why are some of you provoking? No, I do not excuse a man hitting you, and yes, I am aware that there are men out there who just hit women, unprovoked, but I am talking about the Baijan singers of this world who just so happen to (maybe) have provoked a young American singer which led to an exchange of blows, no fellatio. I've always said to myself: what led to him hitting her, what buttons did she push for him to hit her? Or did he just randomly have a Dragon Ball Z moment and flip out on her? I've been out and seen women arguing with their man in public and I sit and just shake my head. The embarrassment alone could stir some form of rage in a man. If you and your man are late for a dinner and it's his fault, why would you feel the need to let the whole dinner table know that it was his fault as to why the two of you are late? Why would you feel the need to tell them that it was his shortcut that made the two of you late?

If you and your man are arguing in the house and it is getting heated and he wants to leave, why would you stand by the door and not let him leave? Why? Under no circumstance am I condoning a man hitting you, but ladies, you have to help yourselves.

There is nothing wrong with being opinionated, as a woman, but no man wants an antagonistic one. Are you antagonising? Do you not know when to let your top lip and bottom lip get married? There is no point arguing with a man when he is upset or angry. His ego has most likely kicked in. His reasoning skills have flown straight out of the window.

Arguing with your man in public, why? Why are you picking a fight in public? What happened to decorum? What happened to the lady in you? This do-it-like-a-dude culture has really got some of you behaving like lager louts. Some of you ladies have to take responsibility in the part you play in provoking some men. Yes, I do understand there are men out there who just hit women, unprovoked, but I am talking about the men some of you provoke. I've had women tell me themselves that they've provoked their man into hitting them. You can't be all up in a man's face, saying, "Hit me, hit me," what kind of nonsensical nonsense? What is the meaning? Why would you edge a man into hitting you? Is your head correct? Please, jump on a bus, go to Billingsgate market, pick up the wettest tilapia you can find, and slap your mouth with it. Why would you do this? Why are you trying a man's patience? In trying a man's patience, you might end up being a patient in hospital, and no, I am not condoning a man hitting you, but some of you have to appreciate the part you play in this matter.

Now, to address the swine that just hit women for the sake of it. I have read many psychological assessments which try to use a troubled childhood as the excuse. Well, sorry, that is no excuse. My childhood wasn't the best, far from it. I witnessed domestic violence; I was beat as a child for being bad. It hasn't made me a woman beater. People will make excuses for any and everything. These immoral moronic morons just like to hit women. I am not buying any excuse, let alone taking it for free, when it comes to a man who hits a woman because she hasn't cooked dinner. That doesn't make sense to me. Is she your slave? Is this Amistad? I am not buying any excuse, I am sorry. I don't care what childhood you went through, you're an adult now, man up. And if you can't do that, don't date. It's not by force. Don't use your troubled childhood as a reason for cracking the rib of a woman. Oh, is it because the Bible told you that G-d took a rib from you that you feel you can crack one? I beg go and sit in the corner, you small boy. You small maggot. I have no ratings for men who just attack women, no ratings whatsoever. I am no saint, but this is one thing I will never accept. There is no excuse. And you women should not stand for it.

A lot of men hit women because they know that the majority of you won't say a thing; they know you will be quiet like bad sex. I have spoken to numerous women who have been victims of domestic violence and I have asked them why they didn't tell their family, and too often, I heard the lines: "Oh, it's my problem, I'll deal with it," or "If I told my dad/brothers, they would kill him." If you stay in that relationship he could kill you. You better scream out like you're having an orgasm and speak up. A lot of men are fully aware of this, they are aware that you will try and deal with it yourself and even if you don't want to tell your family, 999 wouldn't go amiss. I know it's a shame, having to call the police on the man who is supposed to be protecting you, but two tears in a bucket, *fark it*. Call the police on that mofo; yes, dial 999 on his ass.

Why Do So Many Women Stay In These Relationships? Why? Why? Why?

The fear of loneliness. Yes, the fear of loneliness. One of the biggest reasons is the fear that they may not be able to find another knight in shining armour. I mean, in shining tinfoil (excuse the typo). Why would you want to find another man like him? A man that calls you a *bish*, treats you like *craps*, and punches you in the trachea. Why would you? As stated earlier, once your confidence has been stolen, you're well and truly forked.

A lot of women stay in these relationships because they don't want to be deemed a failure; they don't want to have to face their parents and explain to them why yet another relationship has broken down. They don't want the embarrassment. So you'd rather get battered and bruised than face the embarrassment from your parents? . . . Cool. If your parents can't understand why you left, pfffffft.

A lot of women remain in these relationships because they literally have nothing—yes, nothing. It is important as a woman to have your own life. It is important to have some sort of a career. We have moved away from the patriarchal system/times where all a woman was meant to do was cook and clean in the house. Women have been emancipated. Ladies, you have to think of the worse, you have to have your own life. If you don't, you may end up being stuck with a swine.

A lot of women stay because of fear that their partner may actually kill them; some men actually say this to women. They tell them that they will hunt them down and kill them. Sick bastards. The mind games that are involved in these scenarios are deep. But it's a catch 22: you stay he may end up killing you, you leave he may end up killing you. So what does one do?

A lot of women stay in DV relationships because of the kids, as in she may deem it better for the family if he is in the children's life. Well, what about *your* life, honey? How can you raise your kids, living in such a mess? How about your mental state, darling? If he kills you mentally, what use are you going to be to your little cherubs?

It's often the case that the most dangerous time for a woman is when actually trying to leave such situations; even leaving such a situation doesn't guarantee it will stop, as he can come and find her. That is why it is imperative to get the police involved. Make the police aware of what this man, whose brain has been circumcised, is getting up to; shine a light on his dark ways.

Don't suffer in silence; do not, under any circumstance. There are many reasons which could suggest for you to stay, but there is no reason for a man battering you; there isn't any.

If you've hit your man and he has slapped you back—you, as a woman, have to take responsibility for what has happened. No, I am not condoning the act; however, you *did* hit him first. You can't hit a human being and not expect some form of a reaction. Keep your **hands** to yourself, so he can't **palm** off his behaviour. If my sister slapped her husband and he slapped her back and she rang me to tell me, I would ask her *why did you slap him first?* If you are going to attack a man, you can't complain if he hits you back. I am sorry, you can't. As much as Rihanna may make "hit songs", you women cannot live under the "umbrella" that you can do as you wish to a man, hit him and he can't hit you back—as Chris Brown showed. Sorry, you can't. If this is you, cut it out. If you slap a man and he slaps you back, what can you really say?

Men are also victims of domestic violence. There are women out there who actually attack men. Don't for one second sit here thinking you women are **all saints—never ever**. According to the stats taken from the British Crime Survey 2009, for every three victims of partner abuse, two will be female, one will be male. One in six (16%) men (aged 16 or over) and one in four women (29%) will suffer domestic abuse in their lifetime. This equates to 2.6 million men and 4.5 million women. 4.2% of men and 7.5% were victims in 2009/10.

And from what I have researched, men who get hit by women generally feel embarrassed so don't speak out, or possibly don't feel like they'll be taken seriously. Can you imagine a man ringing the police and saying his woman has just slapped him?

Let's not for one second behave like you women are completely innocent, you aren't. Some of you women are just as vicious and malicious as men.

What I will say is this: if your first partner hit you, cool, he was an asshole. If your second partner hit you, okay cool, you met another asshole. If the third partner hits you, sorry, babes, you need to look in the mirror and take some responsibility for what is going on.

There is a difference between a man attacking you and a man who hits you because you hit him. Two different scenarios, so bear that in mind. If you hit him first, you have no ground stand on.

But, as stated, do not suffer in silence. Call the authorities if you are a victim of such abuse. Do not go back if you are dating a man who just lashes out at you. Do not go back to a man who consistently calls you names and puts you down like a wild dog. Do not stand for it. You were not made to be abused, you were not. Like autumn, leave.

If you're looking for a man to complete you,
you've missed the whole point.

Are You Really In Love Or Are You Suffering From Obsessive Compulsive Disorder?

"Don't be so much in love that you can't tell when it's raining."

—*Malagasy Proverb*

As most of us are aware there are four distinct words for love. We have *Agape Love* which is the love 'G-d' is said to have for humanity, which is meant to be unconditional. We have *Philia*, which is said to be friendship or brotherly love. There's *Storge*, which is the natural affection that is felt between a parent and their offspring. And then we have *Eros Love*, which is what one could say is the love/passion that is felt between a couple. This is a step higher than *Philia Love* as this involves a sensual desire and yearning for that individual. It's this form of love that I will be addressing.

I would first like to start off by saying there is evidence to suggest our species has some strong pair bonding modus operandi. However, this is not to say that pair bonding and romantic love are consequently linked. As much as there may be evidence to suggest that the two may be interlinked, and that romantic love is an innate propensity in humans, one has to realise that there is no guarantee that romantic love will endure forever; there is no guarantee whatsoever. It is possible for this love to wear out like those heels that have got your shoes leaning like five past six. In fact, it is said that the most intense stage of romantic love tends to last one and a half years to three years, the rest being autopilot.

Romantic love appears to be a real thing; that feeling, that yearning that one has for their companion. My definition of love is acceptance and tolerance in its entirety. If you can't do that, I don't deem it to be love.

Not everyone defines *Eros/Romantic Love* in the same way. Some have separated it into two different forms: *Passionate Love* (infatuation or limerence) and *Comfort Love* (companionship or attachment). *Comfort Love* isn't automatically void of passion, but centres more on long-term attachment and companionship. *Passionate Love* tends to be more intense and is experienced at the early stages of one's relationship. The period before the novelty wears off, that period when you've got over his sexy body, got over his nice eyes. He is simply Craig now; it's now your friends who tend to remind you how hot he actually is and then you have to remind them to back off like Ghanaian bum-bums.

Helen Fisher and colleagues (2002:415-17), argued that *Romantic/Eros Love* incorporates a consistent suite of traits that cut across cultures. In a sample of American and Japanese respondents (don't ask me why they never chose Nigerians; Kilo Mike Tango) they found thirteen characteristics that they deemed reliably linked to intense Romantic Love, with minor differences between the samples. Here are few of them:

- Obsessive 'intrusive thinking' (You can't seem to get him/her out of your mind).
- Thinking that the other person is unique (Same shit, different asshole).
- Prioritising emotional 'union' over sexual desires. (Don't even get me started on this.)
- Focusing on positive qualities, while overlooking the negative ones (No, he never changed; you just overlooked his misdemeanours because you wanted it to work).

- Increased energy and exhilaration (That buzz you get when you finally meet someone who you deem to be the one. Well, what happened to all the other 'ones'? How many *ones* do you want?)
- A high sense of altruism and empathy towards the person (Putting his desires before yours, going that extra mile to make him smile . . . So why have you stopped?)
- Sleeplessness and loss of appetite (When he's just on your brain and you're enjoying the fiery moments that you spend together).
- Feeling a greater connection to the person during adversity (Until the honeymoon period wears off and it's all guns blazing, even though you're no longer riding shotgun).

To Fisher, the most important out of all of them is "intrusive thinking", because many of the participants felt that they thought about their partner eighty-five percent of the time. *Eighty-five percent* of the time . . .? That sounds like a serious case of OCD. I don't know whether that is a blessing or a curse sent from the deep dungeons of where Lucifer resides. Love does not pay bills, money does. You can't hug your bills and wish they just vanish—nope, sorry matey.

One has to seriously ask themselves whether this thing that one is calling love is not just a case of obsessive-compulsive disorder. I have always thought this. It seems like the most intense stages of *Romantic Love* is similar to an addiction, where each individual can't get enough. Marrazziti et al (1999) noted biological similarities between Obsessive Disorder and *Romantic Love*. It was said that both have a low density of serotonin transporters and involve a fixation on an 'overvalued idea'. Key words: 'overvalued idea'. Hmm, interesting. Very interesting. As interesting as trying to understand why the Sphinxes in Egypt were given a Kelly Rowland—I mean a nose job. Why were they obliterated? I wonder, no Stevie.

Are you aware that there has been some preliminary reporting (Professor Stephanie Ortigue of the Syracuse University) that has found that the feeling of *Romantic Love* can be triggered in the brain in less than a fifth of a second—which would suggest that *Eros Love* is somewhat unconscious and involuntary. That's why I say that there is no point trying to persuade a man to love you. You can't persuade or convince a man to do so, it is something involuntary.

I Think He Loves Me But I Just Can't Feel It

It is said that there are five different ways one can demonstrate that they love someone (DR. Gary Chapman), which means that your man may be showing you signs that he loves you, but you just don't know how to read his language of love. The five different ways are as follows:

Words Of Affirmation

This may be his means of showing that he loves you; his actions may not show it, but this may be his method. The fact that he compliments you all the time. The fact he has a nickname for you. This may be his way of showing he loves you.

Quality Time

He may simply just love being in your company and puts things aside for you, gives you his undivided attention. This may be his way of showing you he loves you. You may not get the 'I love you' every day you wake up; that's because that's not his style. But he may show you he loves you by spending that good quality time with you.

Receiving Gifts

Now, he may not be the type to pay you with compliments, he may not be the type to spend a whole heap of time with you, but his way of showing affection may simply be sending you some flowers to your work place. His way of showing you he loves you may be booking a spa day for you. He may not have the time to spend with you, he may not have a silver tongue that can make you melt, but he may use this method to illustrate his love for you. However, in saying that, one shouldn't assume that a man buying you gifts means he loves you. If a man is loaded, spending money is not a burden. Don't let gifts be a substitute for him spending time with you. When a man is rich, it's his time you need—as it's that, that is dear to him.

Acts of Service

This could be as simple as him helping you with your bags, cleaning up after your mess, anything that is done to ease the burden of responsibility on you. This could be the way he shows he loves you; a man that takes the workload off you. He may not say he loves you, he may not buy you gifts all the time, he may not have the time—but he is thoughtful. This could be shown in simple ways. For instance, you've both gone to a restaurant and it's raining, and he drops you outside the restaurant then goes to find a parking spot. Awwwww, what a Dillon. I mean, sweetheart (honest typo).

Physical Touch

No, this does not only mean sex. This can be as simple as holding your hand when out in public. Public displays of affection, kisses on the forehead, terms of endearment—the fact he gives you massages. This may be the way he knows how to demonstrate his love.

One thing we have to bear in mind is that human behaviour is affected by culture, and *Romantic Love* is no exception. Each individual will have their own ways of demonstrating that they love you, but if after reading the five ways people demonstrate love you're still questioning his love for you, you need not ask him. You already know the answer.

But How Can A Man Who Says He Loves Me Cheat On Me?

A man being romantically in love with you does not stop him fancying other women; it does not stop him watching pornos and getting aroused. Sexual desires may still rally around in a man's cerebellum. I wish people would stop equating love and fidelity as the same thing. I may be in love with you and still stroke a stray cat. For a lot of women they can't detach emotions from sex, so when most women cheat it will most likely mean she has some sort of deep feelings for this guy. When a man cheats, in most cases, it's simply just sex; literally releasing his genes, picking up his jeans and then out in a flash like **Jean Gray**. You can leave a cheat but there is no guarantee your new partner will be any different from your **X-men**. A man can cheat on you and still love you. Yes, he can. His love for you does not diminish the moment he strokes a stray cat. It's imperative that you understand this: when a man is in love with you he will pull out all the stops to make sure he doesn't get caught. For any human being to say that they are hundred percent sure their partner has never cheated is absurd, near asinine. Are you with him/her twenty-four seven? Do you smell his fingers when he walks through the door? Do you tell him to drop his pants the minute he walks in to see if there is signs of residue? Most women are looking for a man who doesn't cheat—when most men do. *Tooo* funny. A man may be faithful and not love you. As stated, fidelity and *Eros Love* are not necessarily interlinked. I could point you in the direction to find a faithful guy, but you've already met him, go get him out of the friend zone. You want to date hot red-blooded testosterone-filled men and expect them to only stroke your cat. Okay, Sally.

A man may show he loves you and demonstrates this through the up keeping of the home and the fact he goes out to work to ensure you have a roof over your head. The fact a man cheated on you does not negate the fact that he may be a good a man; it does not negate the fact that he may take care of the home.

Abraham Maslow's *Hierarchy Of Needs* states five things which are necessary for human survival. It was written in his paper in 1943 called *A Theory Of Human Motivation*. He then extrapolated further on his theory in his 1954 book *Motivation And Personality*. However, it has been argued that fundamental human needs are non-hierarchical and are ontological, as in: don't come in any particular order. However, here are the needs:

The first fundamental need is *Physiological*—that being breathing, food, water, sex, sleep, homeostasis and excretion. What you have here are the basic requirements for humans. Does your man provide this for you? Does he give you sex? Is there food in the cupboards/fridge? Does he take care of the home? Ask yourself those questions.

The second fundamental need is *Safety*—that being security of body, employment, resources, morality, the family, health, property. Does your man make you feel safe? Does he provide enough resources? Is the family well taken care of? Is he a good dad? Does he have a good relationship with the children? These are the sort of things one needs to think about before leaving a man who dipped his nugget in another woman's sauce.

The third fundamental need is *Love/Belonging*—that being friendship, family and sexual intimacy. Do you feel close to your man? Does he involve you in his plans? Do you feel like a family? Do you do things together? What's the sex like? Do you feel like you bond when you're having sex with him? Another bit of food for thought before you decide to walk out of the door because he cheated on you. The perfect man does not exist.

The fourth fundamental need is *Esteem*—that being self-esteem, confidence, achievement, respect of others and respect by others. How does your man make you feel? Does he make you feel confident? Does he respect you? Does he call you names? Does he ridicule you? All these you have to ask yourself before walking out that door. The act of him sleeping with another woman does not negate the fact that he may be a good boyfriend. Pair bonding does not mean one has to be monogamous. Let's not forget that monogamy is unnatural.

The fifth fundamental need, last but not least, is *Self-Actualisation*—that being morality, creativity, spontaneity, problem solving, lack of prejudice and acceptance of facts. Does your man bring out the best in you? Does he allow you to see the good in you? Are you allowed to reach your full potential with him? Does he stub your growth?

So before leaving your man because of infidelity, ask yourself a couple questions: weigh up the good and the bad. Does him having sex with another woman eradicate the years together the two of you have shared? Does his sleeping with another woman negate all the positive things he does?

The woman he slept with—was it a one off? Or has he formed a relationship with her? Is he in love with the other woman? All these questions you need to ask yourself before severing a relationship. It has been said that most women owe the longevity of their relationship to the other woman. Chomp on that for a few seconds.

And if you're still looking for a man to complete you, then you've most definitely missed the point. Now take a trip to Billingsgate Market, pick up the wettest Talapia you can find—and slap yourself with it.

Acknowledgments

I would like to thank all of my friends who helped critique the various drafts of the manuscript. *Lying Fully Clothed: Exposing The Naked Truth About Men* is unequivocally better as a result. Many thanks especially to Lola Adebayo and Jasmine Griffiths who I kept up endless nights as we engaged and battled about a myriad of topics within the book. (Lola, how's that £300 phone bill you incurred? Pahaahhahahaa.) A big thank you to George Kelly, for editing the book; he almost had me in tears with the way he tore apart my grammar and antagonised my ideologies and concepts, but we finally got there.

I also owe thanks to all those who have read my blogs and shared them; it was from my blogs that this book sprung forth.

A cheeky thank you to all the women who have allowed me to break into their heart—but you can't call the police to cardiac arrest me as it was you who let me in. Well, I guess we can all learn from the mistakes we have made.

I owe thanks most of all, though, to my mum, a woman who, through trials and tribulations, stood and raised five kids on her own; a woman who has taught me that you're as limitless as your creator; a woman who, if not for her hard head, I would have been another statistic. I thank you for the man I have become. And last but not least, I'd like to thank my creator, for infinite consciousness.

Lightning Source UK Ltd.
Milton Keynes UK
UKOW051243010512

191771UK00002B/5/P